"These are Two Covenants"

Reconsidering Paul On the Mosaic Law

by Tim Gallant

For these are two covenants: the one, from Mount Sinai, bearing children for slavery: this is Hagar. . . . But the Jerusalem above is free: she is our mother.

(Galatians 4:24b, 26)

Tim Gallant, *These Are Two Covenants: Reconsidering Paul on the Mosaic Law*

First paperback edition: 2012

Cover illustration and design: Tim Gallant Creative
http://timgallantcreative.com

Pactum Reformanda Publishing
Grande Prairie, Alberta
http://pactumbooks.com

Cataloguing Data

Gallant, Tim, 1965-

    These are two covenants

    Includes bibliographical references and index.

    ISBN 978-0-9730119-1-3

    1. Biblical interpretation - letters of Paul. 2. Covenant theology.

      I. Title.

Table of Contents

Foreword

Tim Gallant has done the church a great service by tackling one of the thorniest and most controversial topics in all of theology. There are nearly as many views on Paul's theology of the law as there are theologians who wrestle with the issue. Even in the Reformed tradition, different models of covenant theology vie with one another for supremacy. Perhaps the only point of widespread agreement is that Paul's view of the law is complex and nuanced.

Tim's work cuts through widespread misunderstandings by going straight to the Pauline texts. While Tim is conversant with the ever burgeoning body of literature on Paul's view of the law, he is not beholden to any party or ideology for his views, but rather seeks to engage the relevant passages in fresh ways. He is, first and foremost, a student of Paul himself.

That's not to say Tim is attempting to do exegesis without presuppositions, which is impossible anyway. Tim is coming straight out of the Reformed tradition. But as he puts that tradition in a submissive dialogue with Paul, he is not hesitant to point out areas in which Reformed theology still needs reforming. Many Reformed approaches to Paul's theology of the law leave numerous passages unaccounted for or deal with them only in a highly strained way. Tim's approach focuses on the comprehensive themes of salvation history and eschatology. The result is a wide-ranging, coherent understanding of Paul's theology of the law which accounts for even the most difficult texts with minimal awkwardness. Tim's approach discovers new treasures without losing old ones.

Tim's work is filled with nuggets of exegetical insight. Even those who do not agree with every exegetical conclusion will find Tim's work challenging and insightful. This small book is the product of careful and rigorous scholarship. Tim writes with clarity, charity, and authority. He manages to avoid the heated rhetoric that often accompanies polemical discussion, especially in Reformed circles. I trust his book will withstand scrutiny and serve the church well for many years to come.

In commending Tim's work, I want to especially point to four of its more outstanding features. First, Tim rightly notes that Paul's main focus is not the salvation of the individual sinner. Rather, Paul is concerned with the

5

overarching sweep of salvation history. To be sure, the salvation of individuals fits into that grand scheme. But Romans and Galatians are more concerned with eschatology - the dawning of the new creation in Christ in history - than with the experience of the individual as such. Paul is telling a story, a story that certainly includes personal redemption, but so much more. Tim grabs hold of that larger narrative and shows how Paul views the law as a particular chapter within that story. As one chapter within a wider, longer story, the law is essential yet transitory. It has played its role in the divine drama, and has now moved offstage. The law was a word along the way, not God's last word to his people. In the new covenant Christ alone holds center stage. He is God's final word to the church, and thus supersedes Moses.

The second area of special note flows out of the first. If we really take seriously Paul's claim that Christians are not "under law," what becomes of Christian ethics? Tim's hermeneutical insights into how the old creation law (the Torah) applies in the new creation are of immense value to the church. Paul's eschatological critique of the Mosaic law does not leave us lawless, but rather "in-lawed" to Christ, as Paul himself puts it in 1 Corinthians 9:21. Tim shows that the standard categories of debate are not adequate. The issue is not "continuity" versus "discontinuity," as the theonomy/dispensationalism debate framed things. Rather, the issue is the death and resurrection of the law in Christ. The entire law has been channeled into his person and work, as Tim says. While Moses' Scripture remains authoritative for us, we are no longer under the Mosaic covenant as such. In Christ, we do not so much "keep" the law as we "fulfill" it - with all the eschatological overtones that the term "fulfill" implies. Christ did not simply abrogate the law, but neither did he merely confirm the law as it already existed. Rather, he took the law up into his ministry in order to renew, glorify, and eschatologize it. Tim's insights provide a useful starting point for Christian ethical reflection and practice.

Third, Tim shows how his view of the law's place within the eschatological purposes of God comports with *sola fide*. While Paul would have completely rejected any form of self-salvation (or Pelagianism), we need to be wary of reading later debates back into Paul's letters. There can be no doubt questions of ecclesiology loom large in the Pauline corpus. Paul does more than reject the Mosaic law as a meritorious ladder to heaven, which was never its purpose (even hypothetically) anyway. Rather, Paul rejects the law because it no longer fits with the shape of the covenant community, as that community has been reconfigured and reconstituted in Christ. Tim's work has huge implications for questions such as: Could the Mosaic law be kept by the covenant people? How does the law relate to justification? How does new covenant justification differ from old covenant justification? Is the law divisible into moral, ceremonial, and civil components? What about the traditional "three uses of the law"? Why does Paul reject "works of the law" and yet commend the works of faith? What's the difference? How is the church marked out as the people of God? And so on.

Fourth, Tim touches on aspects of Paul's doctrine of justification that have been neglected or rejected in much of Protestant history. And yet he does so without giving up any ground the Protestants gained in the Reformation. Tim insists that Paul's doctrine of justification is forensic. But we must let the Scriptures define what forensic means, and there is ample evidence that it includes not only a judicial verdict, but also the definitive execution of that verdict. Tim insists that works can never serve as the basis of justification in any way, shape, or form. Nevertheless, the faith that justifies is always a virtuous, working faith. Faith and obedience are inseparable realities. Tim insists that justification is by faith alone. The verdict is issued over us at the moment faith lays hold of Christ. But Paul - and indeed, the Scriptures as a whole - teach that God's final verdict over us includes an evaluation of our life's work. God's final verdict of approbation is itself part of his eschatological gift of salvation, as he crowns and completes his work of grace in us. Tim points to a doctrine of future justification according to works that in no way compromises or subverts our present justification by faith through grace.

Tim's book should be useful to the church as we continue to grope towards a better understanding of Paul's writings. This is not just one more generic contribution in the ever growing library of Pauline studies. Rather, it is a unique and vital entry into the ongoing discussion that lets in new light without shutting out the old. It is my prayer that many will be blessed by Tim's scholarship and that even those who find themselves in disagreement will reckon with Tim's arguments in a respectful way.

Rich Lusk
Tenth Sunday after Pentecost, 2007

Preface

Few discussions in biblical studies have generated as much interest in recent years as that centering around Paul's handling of the law of Moses. The advent of the so-called New Perspective on Paul (NPP) has triggered a great deal of this; but other recent proposals have also contributed.

This little volume is not an attempt to interact directly with the growing mountain of Pauline bibliography. Neither is this an apologetic for the NPP, nor again a studied refutation of it, although some interface is inevitable in the current climate.

These Are Two Covenants is rather less ambitious in scope than such undertakings would prove. It is an attempt to paint a new portrait of Paul's view of *Torah* (the Hebrew for what we call *law*) with attention to features in his writings that are frequently ignored or misunderstood.[1] Although in this little book (an essay, really), I cannot be exhaustive in my treatment of either the entire corpus of Paul's writings, or of the wealth of current secondary literature on the subject, I hope nonetheless that this look into the texts will be found fresh and helpful to all serious students of Paul. Perhaps God may grant that I may take up the more ambitious tasks in years to come.

Credits and acknowledgements

I gratefully salute Rich Lusk, both for encouraging me in writing this essay, and for kindly providing the foreword. His enthusiasm has been a providential motivator.

For gracious consent to review an earlier edition of this manuscript and offer constructive criticism and helpful comments, I owe special thanks to Dr. Nelson D. Kloosterman, Professor of New Testament and Ethics at Mid-America Reformed Seminary, and Dr. Matthew Colvin. Deficiencies, of course, remain solely my own.

Biblical quotations in this book are my own translation unless otherwise noted.

---

[1] On the need for a new reading of Paul, see especially my *apologia*, "Reform for the Sake of the Reformation."

Introduction

"In the letters of our beloved brother Paul," writes Peter, "are many things hard to understand." The difficulty Simon experienced is no less a difficulty for later biblical scholars. Paul's teaching is resonant with multiple layers of biblical allusions, complex patterns of thought, and cryptic turns of phrase.

Nowhere is this difficulty with Paul more evident than in connection with his view of the law. In recent years, books devoted to this subject alone have become so plentiful that even full-time Pauline scholars cannot keep up. Pauline statements both positive and negative concerning the law are wrestled with and a broad spectrum of solutions proposed.

The New Perspective on Paul

A major (but not sole) contributing factor in this torrent of literature has been the advent of the so-called "New Perspective on Paul" (NPP), so coined by James D. G. Dunn in 1982. As many have noted, the designation is not altogether satisfactory. Although there are notable similarities among many scholars within the NPP with respect to their approach to Paul, the real common ground lies in a shared viewpoint concerning first-century Judaism.

This new viewpoint is largely traceable to E. P. Sanders's 1977 work, *Paul and Palestinian Judaism*. This book effectively shook the hegemony of the older view of Judaism, which had crystallized at the time of the Protestant Reformation, and had been further radicalized by German scholars and exegetes of the 19th-20th centuries. This older view asserted that Judaism in the time of the early Church was a religion centered around amassing merit in order to earn salvation. Sanders, however, standing upon the shoulders of earlier scholars such as George Foot Moore, examined a broad spectrum of literature from the Second Temple period. Ultimately, he concluded that first-century Judaism was not a merit-based religion, and was in fact better characterized as "covenantal nomism." Sanders insisted that Judaism must be understood on its own terms as a "pattern of religion," and in order to arrive at a proper interpretation of the data, one must ask the fundamental questions of how one "gets in" and how one "stays in." In answer to these questions, Sanders argued that for Second Temple Judaism, "getting in" was provided for through God's election of Israel, rather than earning one's way. Maintenance within this gracious covenant of election required that one hold fast to the law which God had given Israel.

The matter was not one of merit, much less of perfection; the covenant itself provided means of atonement through repentance and the sacrificial system.

It can be seen from the above that the primary "new perspective" which has developed is not first of all a new perspective on *Paul*, but a new perspective on *Judaism*.

Nonetheless, *Paul and Palestinian Judaism*, it is fair to say, touched off a revolution in Pauline studies. This is so, because a broad swath of texts within Paul's epistles had been read as criticisms of merit theology. It is easy to see that, unless we are prepared to assert that Paul fundamentally mischaracterized his opponents (as indeed some scholars have proposed),[2] full acceptance of the Sanders thesis would entail revisiting the nature of Paul's arguments, particularly those which deal with the law and its relationship to faith.

While there is no single "NPP position" on the reading of Paul, it may safely be said that most scholars who fall squarely within this perspective (as opposed to moderate advocates) have tended to stress that Paul is primarily battling some sort of Jewish exclusivism when he engages in polemics about the "works of the law." The universal gospel of Christ stands over against the law when it is used as a "boundary marker" to identify God's covenant people. The new covenant made in Christ is constituted of Jews and Gentiles, and the law no longer has a role to play in marking out the people of God.

The nature of this essay is not primarily to provide an in-depth analysis of the new readings, which would require a specialized paper devoted to the question. In some cases, it is the opinion of this author that the NPP has helped open up ecclesiological issues in justification which had been largely clouded by the individualistic approach that had come to mark the interpretation of the Pauline texts.

Yet, if we must insist over against many traditional Protestant scholars that the background for Paul's letters is not sixteenth century Roman Catholic theology, but first century Judaism, we must equally insist over against modern scholars that, as much light as historical investigation may throw upon biblical studies, the danger of disallowing Paul to speak for himself is acute.[3]

---

[2] E.g. Heikki Räisänen, *Paul and the Law.*
[3] This caution is quite aside from the disputes among scholars concerning just how far Sanders's

The work that follows, therefore, is neither an attempt to vindicate the NPP, nor yet to re-entrench readings of the various texts that have (rightly or wrongly) come to be viewed as "traditional Protestant" interpretations. What I have provided, rather, is a summary overview of what I see Paul to be arguing concerning the law in various contexts (particularly in Galatians and Romans).

Throughout, I have attempted to derive my interpretation from the structure of Paul's own arguments, rather than through the grid of either a traditional or NPP understanding of first century Judaism. It may be found that the alternatives posed to us (traditional Protestant views[4] versus New Perspective views) in fact are unhelpful. Perhaps, on the one hand, neither side is entirely without need for correction, and on the other, attenuated use of both sides together is eminently possible. Thus, as we approach Paul, it is best to place the NPP debate to one side, and hear the apostle again. He is of age; he will speak for himself.

---

evaluation of the picture of Second Temple Judaism is accurate. On this, see e.g. Stephen Westerholm, *Perspectives Old and New on Paul*, especially pp. 341-51. Note also my comparative review (entitled "Covenantal Nomism?") of Sanders's *Paul and Palestinian Judaism* and D. A. Carson *et al, Justification and Variegated Nomism.*

[4] It must be stressed that the phraseology of "traditional Protestant" is itself very fuzzy. In truth, the Reformation produced many interpretations that have been frequently ignored or dismissed by later generations of Protestant interpreters. Martin Luther, for example, acknowledged that faith itself was counted as righteousness (Galatians 3:6; Romans 4, citing Genesis 15:6), despite the widespread assumption that a "Lutheran" reading would take "righteousness" in this chapter to refer to the imputed righteousness of Christ. Compare Luther, *Lectures on Galatians*, pp. 226-36, which holds together "righteousness consisting in faith" and Christ's imputed righteousness, as complementary, to e.g. John Piper, *Counted Righteous in Christ*, pp. 53-64, which pits the two against each other. While I do not claim merely to be echoing a particular figure from Protestant historical theology, it should thus be understood that much of what sounds "new" in what I present here will in fact have antecedents in the Protestant tradition. This qualification should be kept in mind in numerous contexts where it seems I am critiquing "traditional Protestant" readings.

What Law?

The only way we can discuss Paul's view of "the law" (Greek *nomos*) fruitfully is if we are clear concerning the term under discussion. Is Paul speaking of a universal moral responsibility? All divine commandments? A perversion of one or more biblical covenants into a system of works-righteousness? Jewish oral tradition? We require a generally coherent starting-point before we can proceed.

Particular Versus Universal

One of the difficulties of biblical interpretation lies in dealing with the unseen assumptions we bring to the text. A history of philosophical and theological usage colors how we hear terms. Roman Catholic exegetes, building upon a Thomistic tradition of "natural law" (not to mention "canon law"), understandably have a tendency to hear a universal principle in the term *nomos*. Similarly, Protestant exegetes do their labors within the context of a Reformational dispute which largely took the shape of "law versus faith" or "law versus grace." This dispute had to do with the place of required obedience in the Christian life (i.e. whether it is a basis for acceptance with God etc.).

Nomos thus took on the sense of *all divinely-required obedience*. Thus, in both Roman Catholic and Protestant frameworks, *nomos* tends to be timeless, having to do with supra-historical universals.

Without denying that there may well be legitimate (and even necessary) ways of deriving a secondary application of *nomos* that would approach such usage, responsible handling of Paul requires ascertaining whether for him *law* has such a universal meaning.

I believe that it is virtually impossible to demonstrate that any one usage of *nomos* in Paul's writings refers to a "universal law," and if one such example could be found, it would indeed be a striking anomaly.[5] Paul very frequently places the law into temporal contexts, showing that for him, *nomos* is something that is introduced into history at a particular time. I point specifically to Galatians 3:15-25, which argues that the law was added 430 years after Abraham, was given for a specific purpose, and was

---

[5] Debate rages whether certain instances involve a play on *nomos*, so that in a context discussing the Mosaic law, Paul employs the term as "principle" (e.g. Romans 3:27; 7:21-3; 8:2). The debate in the commentaries is extensive, but for our purposes, relatively little is at stake.

administered through the hand of a historical mediator. Likewise, the apostle clearly identifies Moses and the law in Romans 5:13-4: until the law, sin was in the world, and yet death reigned from Adam to Moses.

Similarly, not only is *nomos* placed in temporal contexts, it is also placed within "national" contexts. In other words, Paul speaks of it as something which *Israel* is under, but not the Gentiles. In speaking of the eschatological judgment, for example, Paul states that God will show no partiality between Jew and Greek (Romans 2:5-11), adding, "For as many as have sinned without law will also perish without law,[6] and as many as have sinned in the law[7] will be judged through the law" (2:12), going on to distinguish Gentiles as being in the former category (2:14-5).

This point, to be sure, is sometimes denied by appeal to Romans 3:19: "whatever the law says, to those under the law it speaks, that every mouth may be stopped, and all the world may become guilty before God." This verse is frequently understood to mean that *the law* stops every mouth, and therefore, the whole world is under it.[8]

Such a reading of Romans 3:19, however, is unsatisfactory. Not only does it come into tension with 2:12, it fails to take into account the preceding context. Paul has dealt already with Gentiles in 1:18-32, painting a picture with which every Jew would agree. But in what follows, he turns to address the unbelieving Jew.[9] Thus, 2:1-3:20 as a whole is designed to place the Jew alongside the Gentile.

Already in 3:3-8, Paul has distinguished between God's judgment of faithless Israel and that of the Gentile world. The Jewish objector suggests that even his unbelief would demonstrate the righteousness of God; therefore, God's wrath against him would be unjust (3:5, cf. 7-8). But Paul counters that on that basis, God could not judge the world at all (3:6). But if the world's condemnation is just (and Paul is implying that God's glory is displayed there too), then what of the Jew (3:8)?

Consequently, Paul introduces his catena of quotations (that run from 3:10-8) this way: "What therefore? Do we [Jews] put forward [an excuse]?[10] Not at all! For we previously charged both Jews and Greeks to

---

[6] Greek *anomôs* - that is, *apart from the polity of the law*. The point is thus not that despite ignorance of the law, the Gentile will come under its judgment, but that the judgment of the Gentile will not be a judgment under the polity of the particular law being discussed.

[7] On the phrase "in the law" (*en nomô*), see the section below, "Scripture and Covenant."

[8] See e.g. John Murray, *Romans, ad loc. cit.*

[9] Putatively, of course - Paul was writing to the church in Rome, not to unbelieving Jews.

[10] Greek *proechometha*; in the middle voice, the idea is to hold something in front of oneself. Thus the issue here is whether possession of Torah or inclusion in the covenant provides immunity from judgment.

be all under sin" (3:9). The apostle is relentless on the disputed point, namely that Jews too are "under sin." This is why, when completing his quotations, he immediately says, "Now, we know that whatever the law says, to those in the law it speaks, so that every mouth may be stopped, and all the world may become guilty [or, accountable] before God." He does not say that all are "in the law." Rather, he presupposes the point established, that the Gentiles are "under sin" and guilty at God's bar. The fact that the charges of 3:10-18 apply to Israel *completes* the picture: all are in this condition; the Jews are not exempt, simply due to possession of the law.

Oral Law?

It is to be conceded that we must watch for contextual clues whether Paul himself introduces something other than Torah into his discussion. Some writers insist that Paul employs *nomos* with a diversity of meanings. Such cannot be ruled out.

Tim Hegg suggests that in the most negative Pauline contexts, Paul is employing *nomos* to refer to the "traditions of the elders," the oral law.[11] He makes a good case that the term is employed this way frequently in the Gospels and Acts. He then wishes to apply this to Paul, which would indeed simplify certain issues.[12]

When it comes to Paul's polemic against law-observance, however, there are serious objections to the notion that the oral traditions are in view. We may only summarize here:

> (1) Whenever Paul polemicizes directly against Torah-observance, his argument always falls within the context of the significance of circumcision, which was mandated by the biblical Torah (see Galatians 5:2, 3, 6; Ephesians 2:11; Philippians 3:3; Colossians 2:11; cf. Romans 4:9-12). Moreover, other practices he mentions are almost always derived directly from the biblical Torah (e.g. Galatians 4:10; Colossians 2:16-7).[13]
>
> (2) Paul's claim that circumcision entails taking up the whole law (Galatians 5:3) does not make sense in connection with the oral law: why would observance of the biblical injunction of circumcision commit one to oral tradition? In any case, this statement parallels an earlier

---

[11] See Hegg, "Can We Speak of 'Law' in the New Testament in Monolithic Terms?"
[12] It is not entirely obvious, for example, why Torah-observance would automatically entail withdrawing from table fellowship with Gentiles (as in Galatians 2:11-4), although deductions from kosher laws, sundry laws regarding uncleanness, and Passover norms are probable factors.
[13] The mention of "the worship of angels" in Colossians 2:18 is difficult, but there is a shift in thought between 2:17 and 2:18; moreover, the oral law did not mandate angel worship in any case.

reference directly out of the biblical Torah (Galatians 3:10; cf. Deuteronomy 27:26).

(3) Paul insists that the Torah he opposes is a covenant (Galatians 4:24), which is ill-suited language to refer to man-made traditions; likewise, he implies that this *nomos* was added in accordance with God's revealed will (see e.g. Galatians 3:19) and indeed is equated with Scripture (3:22).

(4) Paul's analysis of how the problem of *nomos* is solved does not comport with the oral law position. He writes, for example that through the law he died to the law (Galatians 3:19); the oral law, however, was not the instrument either of Christ's death or the believer's deliverance from the law.

Without ruling out *a priori* that Paul *could* have at times addressed oral traditions, we must conclude that such a concern is at most very peripheral in Paul. When he speaks of *nomos* in a Jew-Gentile context, he is not giving particular attention to oral law.

Scripture and Covenant

Nomos in Paul, then, generally refers to the Mosaic law, not to something universal, nor to something specifically rabbinic.

This is not to suggest, however, that every appearance of *nomos* in the Pauline epistles is identical. We must at the very least distinguish between law as *Scripture* and law as *covenant*. The former usage is standard fare both in the New Testament and extrabiblical literature, and can refer not only to the Pentateuch (Genesis-Deuteronomy), but indeed to the Old Testament in its entirety (see Paul's extensive citations of the Psalms in Romans 3:10-18, which in 3:19, as we have just seen, he identifies as "the law" speaking).[14]

The second meaning, law as *covenant*, is admittedly somewhat more difficult, although the extrabiblical literature employs the term with similar frequency.[15] One of the clearest pieces of evidence for this meaning of *nomos* in Paul is Galatians 4:24, which identifies two covenants within a broader context that is very much laden with the *nomos* terminology (cf. also 2 Corinthians 3). Within the immediate context, the verse itself is part of Paul's response to those who "wish to be

---

[14] Cf. also Galatians 4:21: "Tell me, you who desire to be under the law, do you not listen to the law?" Paul goes on to cite the Genesis narrative of the Hagar story, rather than a passage from the "legal" portions of the Pentateuch.

[15] E.g. *Mekilta Exodus* 20:6: "By covenant is meant nothing other than the Torah." Cited in James D. G. Dunn, *Romans* 1-8, p. lxix.

under the law" (Galatians 4:21). It is thus evident that the "law" which Paul is resisting is a covenant.[16]

This covenantal idea is apparently what lies behind the Greek phrase *en nomô* ("in the law," "in Torah").[17] A covenant is a bonded relationship which creates a covenantal sphere. Hence, *in the law* may be compared to Paul's ubiquitous *in Christ* (*en Christô*).

We must, then, distinguish between two prevalent meanings of *nomos* in the Pauline letters. Paul, it is clear, does not quarrel with the continuing authority of Scripture. He *does*, however, deny that the bonded relationship between God and His people established at Sinai bears continuing governmental authority for new covenant believers, as we shall see presently. It is this covenantal usage of *nomos* which is most predominant in Paul and which primarily concerns us in this little book.[18]

---

[16] Thus when Paul speaks of "works of the law" (*erga nomou*), he is speaking of the "works demanded by Torah." So too Schreiner, *Paul, Apostle of God's Glory in Christ*, pp. 110-15.

[17] See e.g. Romans 2:12; 3:19; cf. the essentially synonymous "under law" (*hûpo nomon*), as in Romans 6:14; Galatians 4:21.

[18] It is to be observed that *nomos* as "Mosaic covenant" effectively refutes the charge that Paul has decontextualized the law. While it is true that Paul seeks to disassociate Moses from Abraham (see Galatians 3:15-20), it is not true that for him *nomos* is simply a body of commandments. It is a bonded covenant (cf. Galatians 4:24); Paul never presupposes otherwise. On the appropriateness of Paul's use of *nomos* to refer to Torah, see Westerholm, *Perspectives Old and New on Paul*, pp. 335-40.

Not Under Law

In Romans 6:14, Paul writes, "For sin shall not lord it over you, for you are not under the law, but under grace."

What does Paul mean when he says that the believer is "not under the law?" One thing he cannot mean, given what we have already established concerning the apostle's use of *nomos*, is that the believer has no responsibilities for obedience. "Law" clearly has reference to the *Mosaic* law, not to the Christian calling to obedience.

Another interpretation of Paul's meaning, sometimes put forward, is that the Mosaic law was a covenant which did not proffer grace at all (which would explain the law/grace antithesis in this verse), and that movement from the law would thus entail what we would call "conversion." I do not believe this is what Paul means either.

It is my position that when Paul speaks of not being "under law," he is speaking straightforwardly: *the Christian is not subject to the Mosaic covenant*. Jesus was born under the Mosaic covenant, in order to redeem those under that covenant (Galatians 4:4-5). The point there is not that Jesus knew no grace,[19] and certainly not that all those who were under the Mosaic covenant prior to His coming knew no grace. The point is that His redemption entailed removal from the old order. This is merely a summary of the position; we must now defend it.

Two Ages

Paul's approach to the law is built upon an underlying thought world with a distinctive redemptive-historical shape.[20] His understanding of Torah is pervasively *eschatological*. By this I mean that Paul sees the prophetic portrait of coming glory as having reached an initial but decisive fulfillment in the events of Christ's death, resurrection, the outpouring of the Holy Spirit, and the ingathering of the Gentiles. The time prior to Christ is the age of "flesh," an age which is now passing away. Over against that, the Church is "in Christ," "in the Spirit," and (to borrow

---

[19] Cf. Luke 2:52.
[20] Richard Gaffin summarizes the work of Ridderbos and Vos as concluding that Paul's "primary interest is seen to be in the *historia salutis* as that history has reached its eschatological realization in the death and especially the resurrection of Christ" (*Resurrection and Redemption*, p. 13).

from Hebrews 6:5) has thereby become partaker of the powers of the age to come. Christ's death aimed at delivering us from "this present evil age" (Galatians 1:4); the result is that for those in Christ, there is a whole new creation (2 Corinthians 5:17).[21]

Paul centers this "cosmic transition" in the cross and the resurrection. Christ came "according to the flesh" (Romans 1:3), "in the likeness of sinful flesh," and thus His death was a condemnation of sin in the flesh (Romans 8:3). For Paul, this means that God "executed" the old order of flesh when His judgment was laid upon Jesus. Even as Adam stood as the head of the old creation, under the sway of sin (or better, Sin) and flesh, Christ stood as the head of creation too (see Romans 5:12-21): first "in the likeness of sinful flesh," and then, in His resurrection, as the firstfruits of the new creation. Christ-as-flesh was executed by God's justice upon the cross, but the condemnation was not final; it led to His vindication: He was "justified by the Spirit" through the resurrection (1 Timothy 3:16).

In this way, Christ's history becomes redemptive history: first, He is the new representative of the old creation and is condemned; then He is the representative of the new creation, and is vindicated through the resurrection life of the Spirit. As the prototype of resurrection, He was sown in dishonour and weakness, but raised in glory and power (see 1 Corinthians 15:42-7).

As Paul puts it in Romans 1:3-4, the Son was "born from the seed of David according to the flesh, and appointed[22] as Son of God in power according to the Spirit of holiness, by means of the resurrection from the dead."

This is thus more than an individual justification; it represents and accomplishes the redemptive-historical movement from one age to another. Even as Jesus, being "flesh," was once subject to the dominion of death, and through the resurrection He has been freed from death's dominion (Romans 6:9), so too those in Him are no longer under the

---

[21] On this theme of the "overlapping" of two orders or ages, see e.g. Geerhardus Vos, *The Pauline Eschatology*, pp. 37-41.

[22] As is widely recognized by commentators, the Greek verb *horizō* does not mean "to declare" (as the English versions invariably render it), but "to determine" or "to appoint" (cf. Luke 22:22; Acts 2:23; 10:42; 11:29; 17:26, 31; Hebrews 4:7). This does not mean that Paul does not believe Jesus was Son from eternity; it does mean, however, that in Romans 1:3-4, he is concerned to show that as the incarnate Messiah, Jesus has been appointed "Son of God in power" by means of His resurrection. Even as Adam, Israel, and David and his heirs were representative sons of God (see Luke 3:38; Exodus 4:22-23; 2 Samuel 7:14), the Messiahship of Jesus is a representative sonship. In 1:3, this sonship was still "according to the flesh;" in 1:4, by means of the resurrection, Christ has been appointed to a sonship of power and Lordship over the new creation.

dominion of Sin (6:14),[23] because they are no longer "in the flesh" but "in the Spirit" (8:9). Sin is thus understood not merely on an individual level (various people committing individual sins) - although, of course, that is related - but has reference to a *domain of rule*, corresponding to the weak age of the flesh. Because Christ our Head was put to death in the flesh, the age of flesh (and thus the dominion of Sin) has come to its termination in Him. As Hays succinctly puts it, "The old world has been crucified and new creation has broken in through Jesus' death and resurrection."[24]

This redemptive-historical structure is imperative to grasp in connection with our subject, because Paul places the law within the sphere of the first creation, the *aeon* of "flesh." It belongs to the old order which is done away in Christ. Circumcision, the key marker of and initiation into Torah, is "circumcision of the flesh" (Ephesians 2:11) - a play on words that in fact characterizes Galatians.[25] Being circumcised and observing the works required by Torah is an attempt to be perfected (completed, matured, "eschatologized") by means of the flesh (Galatians 3:2-3). While Israel was under Torah, she was subject to the *stoicheia* - the elements of which the old weak order, the first creation, was constituted. This subjection meant that Israel, although God's heir, was a child living under a slave-like condition (Galatians 4:1-3). Although Torah is itself "spiritual" (Romans 7:14), in that it was given by God, yet it belongs to the old order, to the period of "flesh."[26]

It is in this context that we must understand Romans 6:14: "For sin shall not lord it over you, for you are not under the law but under grace." What initially appears to be a *non sequitur* becomes transparent once it is seen that for Paul, "law" belongs within the old order of weakness and sin (cf. Romans 8:3: the law was weak through the flesh). Paul is speaking

---

[23] Romans 6:9b and 6:14a are parallel: death no longer has dominion over Him (Christ); sin no longer shall have dominion over "you" (believers).

[24] Richard B. Hays, *The Faith of Jesus Christ*, p. xxix.

[25] E.g. the false teachers seek to "boast in your flesh" (*sarx*) by means of circumcision; such flesh-orientation is paralleled with "the world" (*kosmos*) - to which Paul has been crucified, in favor of the "new creation" - in the following verses (Galatians 6:13-5). Cross and new creation are thus juxtaposed to circumcision and "the world" (the "present age of evil," as Paul identifies it in 1:4).

[26] Biblically speaking, Torah is not unique in this regard. The Spirit hovered over the original creation (Genesis 1:2), and even breathed into man the breath of life (Genesis 2:7). Yet the former is not final (a new creation is coming); and Adam is contrasted to the resurrected Christ in terms of "natural" versus "spiritual," in terms which go beyond issues of fallenness and purification to a contrast between initial creation and glorification (see 1 Corinthians 15:44-9). Another way of saying this is that Adam was "flesh" prior to the fall, despite the goodness of his creation, and the Spirit's involvement in that creation. Adam was created with an eschatology - that is, with an anticipation of glorification. Thus too Torah's "spirituality" does not guarantee its permanence as originally given.

redemptive-historically; he is not saying there was no grace under the old covenant. Rather, he is identifying the grace into which believers have come with the resurrection life of the Pentecostal Spirit now made available to those who are united to the resurrected Christ. Awareness of this salvation-historical structure is fundamental to any sound appreciation of Paul's letters, particularly with reference to his view of the law.

Removal from Torah in Galatians

No letter is more marked by Paul's polemic against submission to Torah than is the letter to the Galatians. He is battling against a group of missionaries who have come behind him proclaiming a "gospel" of circumcision. Paul is at his most fiery in his response; this new message is "another gospel," those who embrace it are turning away from God Himself, and those who proclaim it are anathematized outright (Galatians 1:6-9).

Paul's autobiographical narrative in the first two chapters makes it evident that it is submission to the Mosaic law which is at stake. This is why he appeals to his own past in Judaism, when he was extraordinarily zealous for the traditions of his fathers - indeed, zealous enough to persecute the Church which had begun to deviate from the law (1:13-4; cf. Philippians 3:4-6).

The entire letter, then, is triggered by a crisis in *practice*, and not what we might term "theology" - at least, unless we understand "theology" in salvation-historical terms. Paul's appeal to the incidents in both Jerusalem (Galatians 2:1-10) and Antioch (2:11-21) reflect this. What Paul identifies as "enslaving" in Jerusalem has to do with a demand for circumcision (see 2:3); there is no mention of a soteriology (scheme of salvation) of merit, whether elaborate or otherwise.

Likewise, Paul's complaint with Peter is not that he has taught merit theology. In fact, Paul's response is not triggered by *teaching* at all, but by *action*. It is not at all transparent why Peter's withdrawal from table fellowship with the Gentiles would imply "merit theology." The problem which Paul identifies, rather, is that Peter's action is an implicit compulsion of the Gentiles to live like Jews (to "Judaize," 2:14) by adopting the Jewish law - in other words, by coming under Torah.

We must stress that it is not the case that *any* withdrawal from table fellowship would constitute a denial of the gospel. Paul himself mandates precisely just such a separation in the case of sexual immorality (1 Corinthians 5). The problem is not that "withdrawal teaches merit theology;" the problem is that what lay behind Peter's withdrawal was an issue of norms that were peculiar to the Mosaic covenant, a covenant which does not apply to Gentiles under the terms of the gospel of Jesus Christ. Such compulsion is "not walking straightly with the truth of the gospel" (2:14).

It is in this context that Paul employs the language of "justification" in Galatians 2:15-6.[27] "We who are by nature Jews, and not sinners of the Gentiles, knowing that a man is not justified from works of Torah but through the faith of Jesus Christ - even we have believed in Christ Jesus, so that we might be justified from the faith of Christ and not from works of Torah; because from works of Torah no flesh shall be justified."

We will not be able to understand Paul's point unless we recognize both what prompts his statement here, and how he elaborates upon it. This is a thesis statement, and as is often the case with Paul, his thesis statement is cryptic but packed with meaning (cf. Romans 1:16-7). Rather than try to impose a meaning upon it independently, then, we must investigate how Paul himself brings this bud to flower over the course of the letter.

In the ensuing, Paul goes on to argue (2:18) that if he rebuilds that which he has destroyed (i.e. his relationship to Torah), he will constitute himself a transgressor (presumably, because Torah is the sphere where transgression is imputed; Romans 4:15; cf. 5:13-4). Adoption of Torah sets Christ's work at naught (2:21); union with Christ in His accursed death means that one has died to the Torah covenant (2:19; a point to which Paul will return in 3:13).

Paul then adds, "For I through Torah died to Torah, that I might live to God" (3:19). It is to be noted that Paul speaks, not merely of a movement away from Torah, but (enigmatically, to be sure) of a *means* by which this movement was accomplished: *through Torah itself*, he died to Torah. We will see how he envisions this momentarily.

Through the end of chapter 2, Paul has been narrating several stories that lay the foundation for what he is going to say. He has defended the divine source of his apostleship and gospel message (1:10-24); he has likewise defended that gospel as genuinely catholic (2:1-10); and by means of the Antioch incident with Peter, he has provided a tight introduction to the position which he will elaborate in the main body of the letter's argument.

---

[27] Note that "justification" here stands in contrast to verse 11, where Paul says Peter was "condemned" (a point obscured by many English translations). Peter was condemned because he sided against God's justifying judgment. Here the "corporate" element of justification is to the fore. See my online article, "Last Days Justification."

In chapter 3, Paul at last turns his focus again directly to the Galatian situation. Over against the rival missionaries ("Judaizers"),[28] who wish to "complete" the conversion of the Gentiles through circumcision and adoption of Torah, Paul stresses that the Galatians already have full benefit of the covenant. God has already granted them the eschatological Spirit; there is nothing that the "works of Torah" can add to what God Himself has done through the "hearing of faith" (3:1-5).

Instead of supposing that they must convert to Judaism in order to be full members of the people of God ("the children of Abraham"), Paul explains that the Galatians must understand the salvation-historical shape of the Abrahamic promise. He notes first that Abraham himself was reckoned righteous through faith; those who would be his sons will find their sonship precisely "from faith" (3:6-7). The gospel of the Gentiles was preached long beforehand to Abraham, when God promised that all the Gentiles (*ethnê*) would be blessed in him (3:8).

We must catch the import of this: *Gentiles who converted to Judaism were strictly no longer Gentiles, but Israelites.* Furthermore, the Scripture Paul cites says that this blessing involves being *in Abraham*. It is thus no strained logic for Paul to claim that the Gentiles can now be full members of Abraham's people apart from Torah: that was the import of the promise.[29] And now that this is occurring with the advent of the gospel, the Gentiles are blessed "*with* Abraham" (3:9). That is, Abraham is now receiving the fruition of that promise, and the Gentiles are sharing that blessing with him.

It is thus now that Paul arrives at his explanation of why things must be this way - why it is that God inducts the nations into Abraham apart from Torah. The answer is that Torah is itself something from which Israel needed to be delivered. This is the shocking fact which Paul will develop over the course of the next two chapters.

I am speaking particularly of 3:10-14. As this, however, is a notoriously cryptic and difficult section of the argument, I wish at this point to move beyond it for a moment.

It is particularly in 3:15-25 that the redemptive-historical structure of Paul's argument in Galatians is most transparent. Here, Paul stresses that the law was added - indicating a specific historical beginning - and likewise that it served its purpose until the Seed should come to whom the

---

[28] It is has been aptly noted that "Judaizers" is strictly a misnomer; "to Judaize" means "to adopt Jewish customs," not "to force others to adopt Jewish customs." Nonetheless, because the terminology is well-established, we will employ it here.

[29] This combination of factors in the original promise is widely missed by modern critical scholars who imply that the Judaizers probably had a better biblical case than Paul did.

Abrahamic promise had been given (3:19; cf. 3:16) - thus indicating further that it was aimed at a specific historical termination point. Paul adds that during this period, Torah served as a child-custodian (*paidagôgos*) until the advent of Christ (3:23-5).[30]

In 3:15-8, Paul stresses that the Abrahamic covenant antedates Torah. The covenant which God had made with Abraham cannot be nullified, nor compromised by a codicil. Thus if the Abrahamic inheritance entails following Torah, the original covenant with Abraham would fall to the ground: the inheritance would no longer be given by virtue of that promise (3:18).

Given this chronological structure in Paul's argument, it is evident that his concern is not merely with a theological or practical misuse of an eternally valid law; it has first of all to do with the temporary nature of the Mosaic covenant. Paul is not simply saying that one must not try to earn salvation through the commandments;[31] rather, he is showing that the fulfillment of the promises must come about *apart from the Torah covenant altogether.*

We must analyze further the claim which Paul puts in general terms: once a covenant is in force, no codicil or amendment may be added to it (3:15). We have seen that the immediate purpose of this statement is to deny the possibility of simply overlaying the Mosaic covenant upon the promises made to Abraham (3:16-8). But what is widely overlooked is that if Torah is itself a covenant (4:24), Paul must also intend the argument to run the other way (i.e. forward, as well as backward). In other words: *the new covenant cannot be simply overlaid upon Torah.* The new covenant may function neither as a simple annulment of, nor a codicil to, Torah.[32]

---

[30] The Greek word *paidagôgos* has frequently been misleadingly translated as "tutor" or "schoolmaster." The *paidagôgos*, however, was not an academic role. The term refers to the slave who taught basic life-skills to the child and kept him in line. Paul's point in 3:23-5 is not that we ought to use the law to prepare people to accept the gospel (he does not say that the law *leads* to Christ); his point is salvation-historical rather than "pedagogical" in the modern sense of the word: Torah was a temporary institution *until* the faith was revealed in Christ.

[31] An effort, we might add, that Paul would unquestionably oppose: see Romans 4:4-5.

[32] It will be noted that I have intentionally spoken of *simple* annulment. This arises out of a recognition of the complexity of Paul's discussion of Torah. In some places, it appears as if he is speaking of outright abolition. But once Paul's argument is understood in its varying contexts, it turns out that what appears to be mere annulment is in fact accomplished by *escape* (liberation), rather than nullification. Paul says that Christ is the *telos* of Torah *for those who believe* (Romans 10:4). As with the other elements of the old *aeon*, Sin and flesh, Torah remains a reality outside the sphere of the new creation, which is available only in Christ (cf. 2 Corinthians 5:17). The Torah of commandments is "abolished in [Christ's] flesh" (Ephesians 2:15) - strong language indeed: but outside of Christ, it remains a continuing reality.

Consequently, Paul's statement in 3:15 is a compelling argument that Torah and Christ are mutually exclusive. (Lest it be wondered why the new covenant and the Abrahamic covenant are not mutually exclusive for the very same reason, the answer is that Christ is both the content and the recipient [see 3:16] of the Abrahamic covenant, and thus the Christ-event cannot be construed as a codicil upon it. The new covenant is not *another* covenant over against the Abrahamic covenant, but its *fulfillment*. That is why Paul speaks of only two covenants in 4:24, rather than three, as might have been expected.)

It is thus that Paul has laid explicit groundwork for his claim of 3:20: the mediator (Moses) does not mediate concerning the one seed of the Abrahamic promise.[33] Otherwise, both covenants would amount to codicils upon each other.

Such mutual opposition, however, implies somewhat of a problem. If the covenants are mutually exclusive, and yet Torah binds all those under it, a mechanism of removal is necessary. In short, in order to enjoy the benefits of the fulfilled Abrahamic covenant, Israel requires outright deliverance from the Torah covenant.

We have drawn attention above to Paul's cryptic statement in 2:19: "For I though Torah died to Torah, that I might live to God." How is it that *through Torah itself*, Paul has been delivered from Torah?

I propose that we find the answer in 3:10-13. In verse 10, Paul writes, "You see,[34] as many as are of the works of Torah are under a curse; for it is written: 'Cursed is every one who does not remain in all the things written in the book of Torah, to do them.'"

The first order of business is to identify who is being described by "as many as are of the works of Torah." Many interpreters - and even Bible translations - render this, "as many as *rely* on works of Torah." In other words, the people in view are attempting to earn salvation by works.

This, however, is an unlikely reading. For one, Paul simply speaks of those who are "*of* works of Torah" (*ex ergôn nomou*), without specifying anything concerning theological attitude. Further, in verse 13, he will go on to speak of the means of deliverance from the curse specified here. Yet

---

[33] The enigmatic "one" of 3:20 ought to be interpreted through the lens of the previous employment of "one" in 3:16, referring to Christ as the "one Seed" of Abraham. Although I do not follow Wright in his attribution of a collective sense to "Christ," his overall discussion of the passage in *Climax of the Covenant*, pp. 157-74 is profoundly helpful. See also the appendix to my essay, "Abraham's One True Heir?"

[34] Greek *gar*. I am taking this as a marker of clarification, as per the second heading in the Bauer-Danker-Arndt-Gingrich lexicon. The relationship between 3.6-9 and 3.10-14 will, I trust, become clearer as we go on.

no one supposes that his intention in verse 13 is to speak specifically of the liberation of those who had been trying to earn their salvation. To the contrary, 4:4-5 identifies Jesus as being "born under Torah, in order to redeem those under Torah." The most natural way to understand the argument in 3:10, 13 would be to identify "those who are of the works of Torah" (3:10) with "those under Torah" (4:5) - which, at one time, included Jesus Himself!

Galatians 3:10, then, is referring to *all those under Torah*. Unless we take the curse collectively, as applying only on a national level (which strains the language of "every one"), thinking of the curse actively is a difficult option. While an unstated premise ("and no one is able to do all the law") has been read into this verse back at least as far as Chrysostom, two significant problems stand against this reading: (1) perfect fulfillment was never in view in the original text cited; and (2) Paul and Scripture elsewhere freely speak of "blamelessness" according to the law, not because the individual was sinless, but because he remained loyal to the covenant and sought forgiveness through the appropriate means.[35] In fact, according to 2 Chronicles 34:32, there was a time when "the inhabitants of Jerusalem did according to the covenant of God" (ESV), and interpreters are virtually unanimous in agreeing that the "book of the covenant" in question is Deuteronomy,[36] from which Paul cites.

We must expand with regard to the first point. Paul's Scripture proof (Deuteronomy 27:26) is a text drawn from the covenant renewal ceremony upon Gerizim and Ebal. The pronouncement curses all those who do not continue to uphold Torah, who do not maintain covenant. Upholding the law and keeping it perfectly are not the same thing; this is a text cursing those who apostatize from Torah. Thus, if Paul were implying that Deuteronomy 27:26 curses everyone who does not perfectly fulfill every commandment of Torah, his interpretation would run counter to the original intention of the text.[37] I am not convinced that Paul misused original biblical contexts in this manner.[38]

---

[35] E.g. 2 Chronicles 35:26; Psalm 119:55, 63, 69, 100-102, 112, 129, 145-6, 166, 168; Luke 1:6; cf. Philippians 3:9.

[36] This assessment is almost certainly correct; the very passage Paul cites in Galatians 3:10 (Deuteronomy 27:26) seems to be what Josiah alludes to in his confession of national sin in 2 Chronicles 34:21: "Great is the wrath of the Lord which has become inflamed among us, because our fathers did not obey the words of the Lord, *to do according to all the things written in this book*" (translated from LXX; emphasis mine).

[37] It would also run counter to how 2 Chronicles 34 understands Deuteronomy 27:26. (See previous footnote.)

[38] My problem here is not that Paul assigns a universal curse to all those under Torah. Further on in this very chapter, Paul universally consigns the entire salvation-historical period prior to Christ to the dominion of Sin (3:22; cf. also Romans 5-7), subjection to which is doubtless an accursed

There is another resolution - one which requires no unstated premise. It is important to note here that Paul does not say that all those under Torah are *accursed* (Greek *epikataratos*), but that they are *under* a curse (*hûpo kataran*). Following Joseph Braswell,[39] I propose that "under a curse" means: those who are of the law are bound by the curses which were pronounced on Mount Ebal (see Deuteronomy 27:11-26). Those who are *accursed* (not just *under the threat* of being cursed) are those who *break* from Torah.

The upshot is that those under Torah are "locked in" by an oath. This creates a dilemma: the new covenant has arrived, and Israel is bound to the old one by means of an oath. The crisis is heightened rhetorically by Paul in 3:11-2, where he further contrasts Torah and Christ.[40] The tension is only resolved in 3:13: on the cross, Christ has borne this curse against apostasy, thus releasing Israel from the Torah covenant, so that she may inherit the promises of the new alongside the Gentiles (3:14). It is in this way that we understand how it was through Torah that Paul died to Torah (2:19): by means of Torah's own curse-sanction (Deuteronomy 21:23) which Christ bore.[41]

Now we must notice the "so that" of verse 14: the result of Christ's curse-bearing and consequent redemption is in order that (1) the blessing of Abraham might come to the Gentiles in Christ Jesus; and (2) "we" might receive the promise of the Holy Spirit through the faith.

The first of these refers us back to 3:8-9. It is important to stress that it is speaking of a new redemptive-historical moment: because Christ has accomplished the redemption from the curse of Torah in verse 13, it is now possible for the Gentiles to receive the blessing promised to Abraham. As we have seen, this blessing includes incorporation into Abraham, and incorporation *as Gentiles*. This part of the verse, then, flows directly out of our exposition of 3:10-13. Because Christ as Israel's representative (the "concentrated" Seed of Abraham; cf. 3:16) has borne the curse of apostasy from Torah, He becomes representative of Israel

---

condition. The problem here, however, is that Paul has explicitly drawn his "curse" terminology from a biblical passage which is apparently speaking of something else entirely.

[39] "'The Blessing of Abraham' Versus 'The Curse of the Law.'" Quite similarly, see also Gordon Fee, *God's Empowering Presence*, pp. 390-5.

[40] On 3:11-2, see the appropriate subsection in "Why not Torah?" below.

[41] This is not a genuine contradiction of the more popular reading, which understands Christ's curse-bearing to refer to redemption from guilt for *all* violations of the law. The reading here is rather an application squarely based upon that, since apostasy was in fact the ultimate violation against the law. The larger problem is that strictly, only Israel was under Torah; ostensibly, then, the "curse of Torah" did not apply to Gentiles. Israel's priestly-nation status, however, functioned in some way with reference to the sins of the nations, which will be discussed further below.

outside of Torah. And thus the blessing of Abraham comes to the Gentiles "in Christ Jesus." They are inducted into Abraham by being incorporated into Christ, who is now outside Torah.[42]

The second result of redemption Paul mentions in 3:14 is the reception of the Holy Spirit. I happen to believe that "we" here refers specifically to Jews; the point is arguable. Throughout the letter, Paul sometimes employs "you" to refer to the Galatians (3:1), sometimes to Gentile Christians in general (2:5); likewise, he employs "we" to refer pointedly to Jews (most markedly in 2:15; cf. 3:13), while elsewhere it may refer to all Christians, or more narrowly, Paul with his congregations (2:4).

In this particular case, there seems to be intention behind moving from the third-person "Gentiles" to "we": Jews were already incorporated into Abraham in a sense not true of Gentiles heretofore. When Paul speaks of the Gentiles being incorporated into Abraham, however, this is "in Christ," and includes the Spirit as an aspect of that blessing. Thus Paul adds more specifically that Israel receives the Spirit in this same event.

It is not immediately obvious to us why the reception of the Spirit should be dependent upon removal from Torah, and yet it is clear that this is what Paul himself intends. He has spoken of the Spirit as "the *promise* of the Spirit," and thus includes it in the "promises" of which he goes on to speak in 3:16. In 3:15-8, he makes clear that inheritance of these promises cannot come by Torah. We tend to limit that beyond Paul's intent, interpreting his statement to mean merely: these promises cannot be earned by works of obedience. Yet it would seem that the shape of Paul's argument demands something more radical still: *these promises cannot be inherited while Israel is under Torah.* As Paul states it more explicitly in his parallel argument in Romans 4:14, "if those who are from Torah are heirs, the faith has been made empty and the promise nullified." The only way to the promise is beyond the domain of Torah. Even as the Gentiles could not be incorporated into the Abrahamic people as long as that people was under Torah, so too Israel cannot receive the promise of the Spirit as long as she remains under Torah.

I suggest that, at least in part, this has to do with the fact that Paul sees the promise of the Spirit as a new covenant promise, bound up together with the promise to Abraham regarding the Gentiles. As long as

---

[42] This entire line of thought finds a remarkable parallel in Hebrews 13:10-14: Israel under Torah has no right to eat of the new covenant altar (13:10). Christ suffered outside the gate just as the sacrificial bodies are burned outside the camp; the result is that He set apart His people through His blood, that they may go to Him outside the camp (13:11-3). The new covenant people have here "no continuing city" (i.e. Jerusalem), but live outside the camp as seekers of the coming city (13:14; cf. Paul's "Jerusalem above and below" contrast in Galatians 4:25-6).

"Abraham" (i.e. his seed) is under Torah, Gentiles cannot be included in him *as Gentiles*. And as long as *that* aspect of the new covenant cannot be fulfilled, neither can the other. The gifts of the new covenant, for both Jew and Gentile, hinge upon Israel's release from Torah.

As a whole, 3:10-13 falls within Paul's rhetorical strategy to discourage the Galatians from becoming circumcised. Those under Torah - meaning too those who become circumcised (5:3) - are responsible to keep the whole law. It is a "lock-in" situation. It took Christ's death to get Israel out of this dilemma; how foolish, therefore, for the Galatians to enter it!

The shape of Paul's following argument supports this reading. As we have seen, 3:15-25 is devoted to explaining the temporary character of Torah. It is a child-custodian, and through it, all things are in fact "consigned under Sin" (3:22). It is not intended to serve as a child-custodian any longer after the coming of Christ (3:23-5). This is because the *aeon* of childhood has in fact come to an end: those who are in Christ are adult sons, because they have been clothed with the One mature Son. Consequently, they are ready to inherit the promises as heirs of Abraham (3:26-9). During the time prior to Christ, Israel differed nothing from a slave, despite the promise of inheritance. It was under "guardians and managers" (cf. the *paidagôgos* of 3:24-5); Torah belonged to the *stoicheia* of the old creation, to whom Israel was subject (4:1-3).

The resolution is recapitulated in 4:4-5: Jesus was born under Torah, in order "to redeem those who were under Torah," a redemption further defined as the reception of mature sonship through adoption into Christ, a blessing which is shared with the Gentiles (4:6-7).

It should be clear that 4:4-5 articulates the process by which Israel was removed from the guardianship spoken of in 4:1-3. As we have seen, Torah is described in 4:3 as belonging to the *stoicheia*, and Paul specifically employs the term "bondage" in this connection - leading directly to the *redemption* language of verse 5. The particular word for "redemption" employed here (Greek *exagorazô*), note well, is only used by Paul twice with reference to Christ - and the other occurrence is in 3:13.[43]

Given this parallel, we are compelled to say that Galatians 3:13 refers to the redemption of Israel from bondage to the *stoicheia* - that is, from

---

[43] *Exagorazô* is also used (in the middle voice, rather than the active, as here) in Ephesians 5:16 and Colossians 4:5, with reference to believers' redemption of the time. Paul's more common term for soteric redemption is *apolutrôsis* (Romans 3:24; 8:23; 1 Corinthians 1:30; Ephesians 1:7, 14; 4:30; Colossians 1:14); cf. the cognate verb *lutroô* (Titus 2:14).

service under Torah.[44] Once again, this reading continues to be bolstered by Paul's further discussion. The fact that the Galatians have begun to observe days, months, and years in accordance with Torah is to him testimony that they have returned to the "weakness" of the *stoicheia* belonging to the old *aeon*, to which once more they are becoming enslaved (4:9-10). Here Paul parallels the Galatians' former life in idolatry (4:8) with life under Torah. This parallel is made, not because Torah was itself idolatrous, but because, like the idols of the world, Torah belonged to the old age of flesh which is done away in Christ. To turn to Torah is to return to the old creation which they had left behind. It is thus that Paul argues desperately, going into labor in order to rebirth them into the new creation (4:19).

For Paul, the desire to be under Torah (4:21), then, is a desire to be enslaved to that from which Israel had been delivered (4:4-5). Torah is a slave-covenant; she is Hagar, and bears children for slavery (4:24).[45] It was necessary for Israel to live under such slavery during the time of her minority, but now that the Seed of promise has arrived (cf. 3:16; 4:4), those who hold to Hagar rather than to Christ ("Isaac") must be cast out.[46] Those who are in Christ are children of the promise; those who are under Torah will not inherit with them (4:21-31). Christ's liberation has created a new epoch of freedom which must be grasped firmly: for Paul, the traditional Jewish language of "the yoke of Torah" has been transformed into "the yoke of slavery" (5:1), from which only Christ's cross can deliver.

We thus see that Paul's anti-Torah argument in Galatians derives most fundamentally from the conviction that Christ and Torah are two mutually-exclusive covenants. Christ is the new creation; Torah belongs

---

[44] Since Torah is not the totality of the *stoicheia*, redemption from the latter is indeed broader. But 3:13 is speaking specifically of redemption from *Torah's* curse.

[45] Paul's redemption language in 3:13 and 4:3-7 evokes a parallel between deliverance from Torah and Israel's deliverance from Egypt. The fact that Hagar was Egyptian (heavily emphasized in Genesis: 16:1, 3; 21:9; 25:12) may play in the background of the allegory in 4:21-31. That Hagar's son Ishmael was the father of Arabia, in which Mount Sinai stands, helped Paul make even further connections (Galatians 4:25).

[46] It is not to be supposed that it escaped Paul's notice that after earlier identifying Christ as the One Seed of Abraham (3:16), he was here dealing with a text in which God had told Abraham, "in Isaac shall your seed be called" (Genesis 21:12). Underlying the analogy between believers and Isaac in Galatians 4:28 is unmistakably an Isaac-typology which refers to Christ, the ultimate Child of promise. The mention of the one born according to the flesh persecuting him who was born according to the Spirit (4:29) is an echo of Paul's own past: while he persecuted the Church through zeal for Torah, Christ confronted him: "Saul, Saul, why are you persecuting *Me*?" (Acts 9:4). It is Paul's own persecution of the Church while he was under Torah, "in the flesh," which enables him to identify the issues present in Galatia (compare Galatians 1:14 and 4:29).

to the old. This is why Paul says that acceptance of circumcision will make Christ of no benefit to the Galatians (5:2); it is why he insists that turning to Torah amounts to an attempt to be justified by the law - for entrance into Torah is an abandonment of Christ, a falling from grace (5:4). The old order of circumcision/uncircumcision is gone; what matters now is faith working through love (5:6) and the new creation which Christ has brought into being (6:15).

Removal from Torah in Romans

The epistle to the Romans is a great deal lengthier and more complex than Galatians. Since this essay is not intended as a comprehensive exegesis of everything Paul says on our subject, we cannot here run through this letter to the same degree as we did the earlier epistle. Thus, while we will come back to various passages in Romans at numerous points in the essay, we will focus here upon the passage where removal from the law is articulated most clearly.

We have already noted that in 6:14, Paul has insisted that believers are "not under Torah, but under grace." This conviction had been hinted at earlier, but not developed. Back in Romans 4:14-5, Paul writes: "For if those from Torah are heirs, faith has been emptied and the promise nullified. For Torah works wrath; for where Torah is absent, neither is there transgression." It can scarcely be doubted, then, that the "promise" of which Paul speaks (in context, that Abraham would be heir of the world, 4:13) will not be fulfilled under the Torah covenant. As with Galatians 3:6-9, 15-8, the Abrahamic blessing must find fruition beyond the realm of Torah.

As concerns a mechanism of release from Torah, however, Paul makes no explicit mention in Romans until 7:1-6. Here, as in Galatians 3:13, the mechanism is the cross.

This passage is frequently treated as a description of the movement of an individual from darkness to light. To "die to the law" means, to die to the "covenant of works" and be made alive in Christ, or something similar. The argument is thus placed squarely and solely within an *ordo salutis*, rather than within the context of salvation-history.

One feature of the passage, however, indicates clearly that Paul is speaking within a salvation-historical framework, rather than dealing only with individual conversion. In verse two, he writes that a woman is bound by the law of her husband as long as he lives; if he dies, she is released from "the law of her husband." In verse three, Paul adds: "Therefore, if while the husband lives, she will be called an adulteress if she becomes married to another man; but if the husband dies, she is free from that law: she will not be an adulteress, though she has become married to another man."

Here we see that the issue for Paul is not simply the law's condemning *power*. For the issue in such a case would never raise matters of *legality*, as Paul does here. The unbeliever would never be identified as an "adulteress" for leaving such a supposed law-relationship; rather, the unbeliever would simply be *unable* to escape. Paul, however, is concerned with the *legal right* to abandon Torah.[47]

Despite frequent failure of commentators to find theological significance in 7:2-3, Paul surely intends to draw theological significance from these statements: he opens verse 4 with a *therefore*. "*Therefore*, my brothers, you also have become dead to Torah through the body of Christ, *so that* you may be married to another." The *permissibility* of being married to "another" (Christ) is grounded in Christ's death, in which a multivalent death of the believer and Torah has taken place. (The crucifixion of Torah implied here is analogous to Galatians 6:14; even as the death of the world upon the cross does not destroy the old creation world, but makes it "dead" with reference to those who belong to the new creation, so too Torah's crucifixion does not simply abolish it, but makes it "dead" with reference to those in Christ.)

This passage, consequently, is specifically directed to Jews and proselytes. As he has said in verse one, Paul is here specifically speaking to those who "know the law," and in particular, Jews. He is not assuming here that Gentiles were ever under Torah; rather, he is describing the process by which Jews were enabled to move from Torah to Christ. They had been married to the law, but through death they died to the law and are now united to Christ. Because of that death (whether we focus upon Torah's death,[48] the believer's, or both), there has been no violation of the "law of the husband" in the believer's abandonment of Torah. Its hold has been broken in Christ's representative death in which both Torah and believer died in some sense, so that the Jew may move forward into the new *aeon*, the new age of the Spirit inaugurated in Christ.

---

[47] Given his assumptions concerning continuity, it is not surprising that Murray provides no exegesis for verses 2-3. He merely claims that "it is quite arbitrary to subject them to allegorical interpretation. . . . The facts stated need no exposition" (Romans p. 240). That Paul wrote two wasted verses (on Murray's reading) should have alerted Murray that he was on the wrong track. Hodge (Romans p. 216) likewise finds no theological significance here.

[48] As in Ephesians 2:15: Christ "abolished . . . the law of commandments contained in ordinances;" cf. Colossians 2:14, where Torah's "handwriting of requirements" is nailed to the cross - i.e. crucified.

It may well be objected that such a focus upon Jews would be inappropriate to a largely-Gentile church. This, however, imposes modern rhetorical sensibilities upon Paul, and ignores the fact that throughout most of the first half of the letter, his dialogue has been with Israel (see especially chapters 2-4). The plight he describes in 2:1-3:20, in particular, is driving toward resolution in Christ; it is thus not so surprising that he focuses upon the Jews in the church as he reaches his denouement.

This passage once again presupposes Paul's fundamental principle developed in Galatians, namely, that Torah and Christ are mutually exclusive covenants. Being in Christ entails having died to the old *kosmos*, including Torah. Inclusion in the new covenant age of grace necessarily means that one is no longer under Torah (Romans 6:14). This movement is a signal blessing, because Torah belonged to the old age of "flesh."

There is, however, an apparent difficulty with this analysis. For Paul's statements do not always appear altogether consistent. It is in this very letter that he has written: "Do we then nullify the law through faith? Impossible! To the contrary, we *establish* the law" (Romans 3:31). How can Paul both *establish* the law, and insist that believers have emerged out of it into the new creation?

There are multiple levels to the answer, and we can only provide a brief sketch at the moment. With regard to 3:31, the most important thing to notice is that already in 3:21, Paul has drawn attention to the distinction between *being under Torah*, and *receiving its witness*: "But now apart from Torah the righteousness of God has been revealed, borne witness to by Torah and the prophets." As we have already seen, Paul sometimes plays with *nomos*, alternating the sense of *Mosaic covenant* and *Torah as Scripture*.

That this is the primary issue in 3:31 is rendered probable by *how* Paul "establishes the law" in what follows (a point frequently lost because readers give too much weight to chapter breaks). In 4:1, Paul asks, "What *therefore* shall we say that Abraham our forefather according to the flesh has found?"[49] The entirety of chapter four is an exposition of the narrative portion of Torah, with illustration from a psalm of David: thus, "the law and the prophets" which bear witness to the righteousness of God (3:21). Consequently, when Paul establishes the law, he is far from securing the continuing validity of the Mosaic covenant. To the contrary, in this very context, he insists that those who are of Torah cannot be heirs of the

---

[49] Alternatively, "What has our forefather Abraham found according to the flesh?" That is, did he find righteousness *kata sarx* (according to the flesh), or by transcendent grace?

promise (4:14). Thus, Paul's purpose is to show that the witness of all Scripture has come to full fruition: *this* is how he establishes the law.

It is to be admitted, however, that there are further ways in which we may speak of an "establishment" or "fulfillment" of Torah. We will comment later on the issue of how Torah becomes "fulfilled" in Christian ethics. We must also add that the Mosaic covenant itself finds a sort of "realization" in the new covenant: the death of Christ, in which Sin is condemned in the flesh, amounts to a fulfilling of the righteous sentence of Torah (Romans 8:3). It is Christ to which Torah points as its goal (10:4). These reflect complex issues of continuity - but in no case may we speak of the Torah covenant being adopted as part of the new covenant. New creation believers are not under Torah.

Torah Nailed to the Cross: Ephesians and Colossians

Two other related passages speak of the cross as the means by which the law loses its power over believers: Ephesians 2:14-6 and Colossians 2:13-4. In both these contexts (unlike in Galatians), Paul is primarily addressing the Gentile perspective, rather than the Jewish one.

Prior to the Christ-event, the Gentiles were "the uncircumcision" and alienated from Israel, but have now been brought near through the cross (Ephesians 2:11-3; Colossians 2:11). How has this occurred? Christ has become peace between Gentiles and Jews, by breaking down "the middle wall of separation, the enmity, having abolished in His flesh the law of commandments consisting in ordinances," with the result that from two (Jews and Gentiles) He could create one new man (cf. Galatians 3:28), reconciled to God "in one body through the cross" (Ephesians 2:14-5).

In the language of Colossians, Christ "erased the handwriting in ordinances which was against us" by "having nailed it to His cross" (Colossians 2:14). In this case, Paul's first-person plural ("us") appears to be set over against the second-person plurals in the context. That is, Paul addresses the Colossians as Gentiles, and employs "us" for "we Jews." The commandments of Torah came to be "against us." He does not explain how this is so; given the Jew-Gentile context here, which stresses the new unity between them, Paul may well be underscoring how Torah barred Israel from the promise to Abraham, that all the nations (Gentiles) would be blessed in him (cf. Galatians 3:8).[50] At any rate, as we have seen, Paul sees Torah as belonging to the old *aeon*, as among the

---

[50] Paul is thus not saying that Torah's commandments are against Christian believers, but describing how the law functioned as a barrier between the Gentiles and the covenant community, and consequently between Israel and the Abrahamic promise to inherit the nations.

stoicheia of the old creation (see now 2:20 here in Colossians; cf. Galatians 4:3), and thus in principle it stands outside the new creation.

Although Paul's formulation in Ephesians and Colossians is considerably different than in Galatians (and, for that matter, Romans 7), the fundamental issues involved are nonetheless constant. In neither case is it simply possible to "move beyond" the law; it requires the very death of Christ to accomplish the transfer. The result is that Gentiles and Jews can be joined together without coming together under Torah; this constitutes a disarming of the "principalities and powers," in which Christ triumphs over them (Colossians 2:15).[51]

Other Pauline Statements on Removal from Torah

That this movement from Torah to Christ (as mutually-exclusive covenants) is Paul's fundamental position is reflected in how he views himself. He *became* as one under law when he was among those who were under law (1 Corinthians 9:20). His Torah-observance among Jews was thus a practical condescension, but his own self-understanding was that he himself was not under Torah. It was a covenant to which he no longer belonged.[52] Speaking to Gentiles, he says that he has "become as you are," and thus urges them to imitate his own disavowal of the Torah covenant (Galatians 4:12).

This helps shed light on the much-controverted statement in Romans 10:4 that Christ is "the *end* of the law" (Greek *telos nomou*) for those who believe. There has been much dispute regarding whether *telos* ought to be translated as *end* (as in the sense of *termination*), or as *goal*. This dispute has generally obscured the fact that even *goal* can imply some sort of termination. If Christ is the goal of Torah, then the arrival of Christ means that it has fulfilled its purpose. If you travel a highway to a certain destination, that place is your goal. Having arrived at the destination, the highway has served its purpose for the journey. Thus when Paul writes that Christ is the goal of Torah, he is saying that it has served its redemptive-historical purpose. One no longer travels upon the road of Torah, because the destination of that road is now present. New covenant believers are not under Torah.

---

[51] It appears that this refers to Christ's victory over the *stoicheia* of the old creation, which have been disarmed through Christ's suffering in the flesh. In addition to my comments above on the "two ages," note especially N. T. Wright, *Colossians and Philemon, ad loc. cit.*

[52] This mention of Paul's own practice raises the issue of how a doctrine of mutual incompatibility between the covenants can be harmonized with the fact that Jewish Christians largely remained Torah-observant. For a brief discussion of this question, see the chapter "Jewish Christians and a Defunct Law," below.

Another striking passage which we cannot fully develop here is 2 Corinthians 3, with its powerful contrast between the ministry of the new covenant and that of the old. Notwithstanding Scott Hafemann's valiant effort to preserve the law from being subjected to "passing away,"[53] Paul's intentional "new covenant" terminology itself implies the obsolescence of an "old covenant," represented in the passage as "the ministry of death." It is indeed true that turning to the Lord results in the veil being taken away from *the old covenant* (3:14-6). It is mistaken, however, to understand this in a static sense of a long-awaited realization of the meaning of an unchanged law. Rather, as we have just seen, Torah itself finds its goal in Christ (Romans 10:4). That is why, when the veil is removed, it is not the fading glory of Moses which is beheld (cf. 2 Corinthians 3:7-11), but the glory of the Lord (3:18).

In other words, *the new covenant is not simply another way of looking at the old covenant.* The new covenant is the eschatological revelation of God's righteousness in Jesus Christ, accompanied by the Spirit of Pentecost, which creates a new situation, introduces a new *aeon*. As Paul will say shortly, "Therefore, if anyone is in Christ - a new creation! The old has passed away; behold, the new has come" (2 Corinthians 5:17).

[53] *Paul, Moses, and the History of Israel, passim.*

Why not Torah?

To this point, we have already seen strong evidence that Paul's view of the law is highly complex. We need to go further to understand the vigor of Paul's apparently negative view of Torah. In order to get at this, we must recognize two strands of problems. The first has to do with how Gentiles stand in relation to Torah; the second, how Torah itself is to be understood in its own weakness and temporality (i.e. leaving the Gentile question aside). We will take these issues up in turn.

Gentiles and Torah

Whatever we may say regarding Israel's motivation for rejecting Christ (and without question it did have to do with misplaced reliance upon Torah),[54] in the case of the Judaizers it does not appear that Paul is battling merit legalism.[55] Within the context of the Church, both Acts and Galatians (as well as hints in other letters of Paul) reveal that the central law-related problem in the first century Church revolved squarely around one point: *Do Gentiles need to become circumcised in order to be saved?* In order to understand the significance of this question, we need to step back and gain perspective.

In terms of Old Testament norms, full membership in Israel was never strictly an ethnic issue. This becomes clear, for example, in Exodus 12:43-9. There we learn that if a non-Israelite wished to participate in Passover (thus identifying with Israel's exodus-history as his own), he needed to become circumcised, along with his household. The result would be that no longer any distinction would obtain between him and ethnic Israelites; "he shall be as a native of the land" (Exodus 12:48). A careful reading of the Old Testament reflects this fusion; many Israelites have completely "Gentile" roots. When they became circumcised, they were incorporated into Israel and simultaneously enrolled into the Mosaic

---

[54] This is implicit, for example, in how Paul identifies boasting in God and Torah as characteristic of present Israel (Romans 2:17, 23), only to critique such boasting (3:27-30), and reorient it in Christ (5:2, 3, 11). More on this theme below, in the section "Israel's Boast."

[55] We must be careful, however, not to confuse the concerns of Galatians and Romans. Too many NPP interpreters appear to read Judaizing sorts of issues into Romans, a letter which is dealing, not with attempts *within* the Church to impose Torah upon Gentiles, but with an apologetic in the direction of unbelieving Israel. Romans is not Galatians.

covenant to which Israel was subject.[56] *These "converts" were therefore no longer Gentiles.*

In addition to these, however, there were always Gentiles who never became incorporated into Israel, but nonetheless believed in Israel's God. We could cite Naaman as a prime example: although he clearly converted to faith in Yahweh, Elisha made no suggestion that he was required to become circumcised or observe Torah (2 Kings 5:1-19). In fact, uncircumcised Gentiles were even allowed by the law to present grain and drink offerings at the tabernacle or temple on the same footing as a full Israelite (see Numbers 15:14-6 in context). As well, an entire Old Testament book is devoted to a Gentile: Job.

This situation continued into the first century, which is why we find records of Gentile "God-fearers" (e.g. Cornelius in Acts 10) who sustain various sorts of relationships to Jewish synagogues without being circumcised. Such God-fearers, however, had already become the object of growing controversy. Some Jews had become so Torah-focused that they were insisting that proper conversion necessarily entailed circumcision and observance of Torah.[57]

As we have seen, this controversy carried over into the fledgling Church. Many Christians of the circumcision party insisted that Gentile salvation required circumcision and Torah-observance. It is conceivable that some Judaizers were more modestly suggesting that first-class citizenship in God's new people required circumcision (upon the analogy of Judaism, which admitted proselytes into Israel, but also had God-fearers on the "fringes"). Yet it seems more likely to me (not least due to the corroboration from Acts) that both Paul and his opponents recognized that the kingdom age, in keeping with the great Old Testament prophecies of a coming age of *shalom*, was to be characterized by closeness of fellowship between Israel and the nations (cf. e.g. Isaiah 2:1-4, which speaks of the nations coming up to Jerusalem to learn the law).[58] Thus the Judaizers may have supposed that the Messianic era was one in which the Gentiles would convert *en toto* to the Mosaic law in order to facilitate such fellowship.[59]

---

[56] Cf. *Letter of Aristeas* 14.10: a circumcised convert is "incorporated into the house of Israel forever."

[57] See, for example, Josephus, *Antiquities* 20:44-5.

[58] The question arises how Paul himself would have seen such prophetic texts. Given our earlier observations regarding 1 Corinthians 9:21, where Paul identifies himself as *ennomos Christou* ("in-lawed to Christ"), it seems likely that he understood "law" in Isaiah 2:1-4 eschatologically, as referring to Christ Himself. See further comments on "Christ as Torah" in the next chapter, "Justification, Torah, and the Abrahamic Covenant."

[59] It is to be remembered that Jesus' ministry centered the kingdom around table fellowship,

The contention of the Judaizers in Acts 15:1, 5 raises the question for the Church: *Do Gentiles need to become circumcised in order to be saved?* Because we live in an intentionally desacralized culture, we automatically hear "works righteousness" in that question. "Aha! Salvation by the work of circumcision!"

Reading merit into the Judaizers' position, however, is probably a substantial over-reading of the text. The simplest reading is merely that this group considered salvation to belong strictly to the Jews (cf. John 4:22), as defined by Torah. Moreover, as Rich Lusk has pointed out, if circumcision and the keeping of the Mosaic law are considered meritorious in Acts 15:1, 5, then we must concede that the Jerusalem council's response views the minimal requirements (abstaining from idols, sexual immorality, things strangled, and consumption of blood: see Acts 15:19-20, 28-9) as likewise meritorious.[60]

This absurdity suggests that we have placed the entire episode upon the wrong footing. The real issue is not one of merit; the real issue is that in the judgment of the council, the Pharisee-group has imposed Israel-specific laws upon Gentiles. (The "minimal requirements" of the council were not in fact "Torah-lite," as is often supposed, but appear to be primarily drawn from Leviticus 17-8, referring to matters that were applicable to "strangers" as well as to Israelites.[61] Thus the council apparently appeals to Torah itself to reject the necessity of Gentiles coming under the Torah covenant.)

We can get a clearer picture from another angle. If "circumcised" is swapped with "baptized" in the question ("Do Gentiles need to be *baptized* in order to be saved?"), the apostolic answer would have been a resounding "Yes!" Yes, Gentiles and Jews need to become baptized in order to be saved (cf. Acts 2:37-8). The kingdom is given to those who are born of water and Spirit (John 3:5).[62]

My point is that Paul's problem with circumcision is not that it is a *sacrament*. Nor is his problem that a sacrament is being connected to *salvation*. Rather, his problem is that it is an *initiatory sacrament into the*

---

which made Torah-observance a more acute problem than it may otherwise have been.

[60] Rich Lusk, "Getting the Galatian Heresy Right."

[61] The council forbids idolatry, eating blood and things strangled, and fornication (Acts 15:20, 29). Leviticus 17:8-9 (mandating offerings to Yahweh alone, at the appointed place) is related to idolatry; eating blood and strangled things is prohibited to strangers who dwell in Israel in Leviticus 17:10ff.; fornication is forbidden in Leviticus 18 as an act abominable among the nations. See Jordan, "New Testament and Dietary Laws," pp. 24-7. Cf. also Dunn, *Acts*, p. 204.

[62] *Contra* Sanders's inexplicable statement, "Paul would doubtless have opposed any other form of initiation as vigorously as he did circumcision" (*Paul, the Law, and the Jewish People*, p. 158).

wrong covenant. More than this, it is an oath-bound sacrament that commits one to that covenant in total (and permanent) fashion. And this is a fundamental issue for him, precisely because one must choose *between* the covenants. It is *Torah or Christ.*

Once more, this is apparently why Paul writes that the one who becomes circumcised thereby becomes "a debtor to keep the whole law" (Galatians 5:3). Circumcision may seem like a convenient way to escape persecution from the synagogue (Galatians 6:12; cf. 5:11), but it enrolls one in a covenant which demands comprehensive upholding of Torah. (Meaning, among other things: sins are ostensibly forgiven through the old covenant cultic rites, and the laws effectively separating Israel from the Gentiles must be maintained.) Given this, for Gentiles to become circumcised is a *nullifying of the work of Christ* (cf. Galatians 2:21).

This brings the issues of justification and righteousness in Galatians 2:16 into sharper focus. Whatever else may be said concerning that passage, it is clear that the antithesis between Christ and Torah throws those under Torah wholly upon their own works.[63] While there was a time in which Torah served alongside the Abrahamic covenant (as is implied in Galatians 3:15ff.), the crisis point has arrived. The Abrahamic covenant has been taken up in the coming of "the faith" (cf. Galatians 3:25), leaving Torah as a prison without a redeeming purpose.

It can be said in summary that in Paul's view, his opponents (1) were out of step with Israel's past, in that they thought salvation could come only within the Torah covenant, which was never intended for Gentiles; and (2) were out of step with the cosmic significance of the Christ-event: the new creation posits a radical choice between Torah, on the one hand, and Christ as God's eschatological salvation, on the other.

Why and Wherefore

In the foregoing, it has become clear that Torah and Christ are mutually incompatible covenants. We have seen that Paul understands Torah to have been an agent that "locked in" all things under the old *aeon.* Thus one aspect of the new creation in Christ is deliverance from Torah.

So much is clear enough, but the fundamental critique of Torah which underlies it is less so. Can we go further than simply stating *what* is the case (Torah belongs to the old creation), and explain *why* it is the case (why it is that Torah belongs to the old creation, and *only* to the old creation)? Does Paul's repudiation of the law imply that in some way

---

[63] It is to be noted, then, that even if we completely dispel the merit issue from Galatians, Paul's position necessarily excludes any notion of human righteousness upon the basis of human works.

God's purpose with it has failed, or that there has been divine confusion or indecision?

The last idea may be rejected out of hand. While Torah must now give way to Christ, this is not because God has changed His mind. Redemptive history is not a simple, straight line; but neither is it confused or self-contradictory. Torah plays a necessary and important role in salvation history.

The fact, however, that such questions are raised should not disturb us. For within Paul's own arguments, he too is aware that he is raising just such questions concerning Torah's purpose. A clear example of this is Galatians 3: immediately after arguing that Torah is not intended to be the means of receiving the promise (3:15-8), Paul asks rhetorically, "Why the Torah, then?" (3:19). He senses what his line of argument would naturally suggest to his hearers.

Paul's answer is that Torah was added "for the sake of transgressions," which most interpreters (rightly, I believe) now take to mean, "for the purpose of *increasing* transgressions," or at least: "for the purpose of *marking out sin* as transgression."

The Greek word *charin* has two primary meanings, having to do with (1) *purpose* or *goal*; or (2) *reason why*. Thus Galatians 3:19 could mean that Torah was given (1) *for the purpose of introducing, multiplying, or strengthening transgressions*; or (2) *on account of transgressions*. The latter would imply that Paul is focusing upon Torah's function in restraint of sin, means of atonement, etc. The context, however, pays no attention to sacrificial or atonement issues, and although the discussion of the *paidagôgos* in 3:24-5 may lead us to think of sin's *restraint*, that is not in fact the point which Paul draws from the role of the child-custodian. Rather the opposite is the case: by means of Torah, "Scripture has imprisoned all under Sin" (3:22). This is paralleled in 3:23 with being imprisoned under Torah, which in turn leads into the identification of Torah as *paidagôgos* in 3:24. Thus, *in this context,*[64] Paul's view of Torah is not dealing with the restraint *of* sin, but confinement *under* Sin. Paul frequently makes similar remarks: "Torah entered, *so that* the trespass might increase" (Romans 5:20); "the strength of Sin is Torah" (1 Corinthians 15:56).

To this point, our most extensive exegetical investigation has been in Galatians, and there Paul provides little expansion upon his meaning. It is not until we reach Romans that Paul articulates a fuller view of the underlying issues. This is not entirely surprising. Galatians is an *ad hoc*

[64] As opposed to, say, 1 Timothy 1:8-11.

response to Christians who are in the process of Judaizing; moreover, these are churches among whom Paul has labored. Thus, a great deal can be presupposed. Romans, on the other hand, while it is hardly the systematic-theological treatise it is sometimes made out to be, is nonetheless a more structured exposition of the hope of Israel, set over against her unbelief, and in particular her fixation upon the works of Torah in such a manner that she has not recognized the righteousness of God in Christ. Moreover, Paul is writing to a church he has never visited (cf. Romans 1:10, 13); there is much less that can be taken for granted. Consequently, in this letter, matters which elsewhere remain somewhat submerged come further to the surface.

Life Under Sin

Paul's most extensive development of the theme of "life under Sin" belongs, unfortunately, to one of his most disputed passages: Romans 7.7-25. We are tempted to blink when our exegetical tradition has almost universally read the passage one way, and Paul's train of argument leads us another way, but we must not.

The argument concerning Romans 7:7-25 was historically a dispute over whether the "I" referred to an unbeliever or a believer. The Reformed and Lutherans have generally recognized, rightly, that an unregenerate man cannot truly hate sin (7:15) or delight in the law of God according to the inner man (7:22).[65] Thus, Paul must be speaking autobiographically, as the first-person present tense suggests.

On the point of delight in the law of God, I am in full agreement with the Reformed tradition on the inability of the natural man. But it should be clear from our reading of Paul so far that it is a mistake to read him as if he were discussing "timeless truths." Romans, like Galatians, is a sustained salvation-historical argument. Framing the question in the abstract as "believer" versus "unbeliever," as if there were no possibility of distinguishing between eras of salvation history, places the discussion on the wrong footing before the interpretive process has an opportunity to begin its work.

We may identify three reasons that may plausibly be used as evidence that Paul is writing his "Christian autobiography" here. Alongside the grammar (first-person present tense) and the mention of delight in God's law (7:22) already noted, there is also Paul's exclamation in 7:25. "But

---

[65] E.g. John Calvin, "Commentaries on the Epistle to the Romans," p. 265, commenting on 7:15: "Paul speaks here of the faithful, in whom the grace of the Spirit exists, which brings an agreement between the mind and the righteousness of the law; for no hatred of sin is to be found in the flesh."

grace to God through Jesus Christ our Lord!" This exclamation is followed by a restatement of the foregoing: "Therefore indeed, I myself in the mind serve the law of God, but in the flesh, the law of Sin." Given this juxtaposition, it is often thought that life in "Jesus Christ our Lord" must be concurrent with the following summary. The struggle is the struggle of the Christian believer.

These reasons, however, are not as substantial as they may at first appear. Although this passage is unusual, in that Paul employs a first-person present tense to refer to something beyond his own present experience, there are other factors to consider. First is that Paul has a strong identification with Israel and her history, such that in 9:1-3 he is on the point of anathematizing himself on behalf of his kinsmen, were such possible. Paul is fully engaged with the *pathos* of life under Torah, and we must not restrain his rhetoric to fit our own conventions.

Second, Paul does employ the first-person present tense earlier in the letter - however briefly - to refer to something that is *not* his present experience. In 3:7, he asks, "Now, if the truth of God by my lie abounds unto His glory, *why am I yet judged* as a sinner?" As careful comparison between 3:5 and 3:25 will show, in the context Paul is speaking of how Israel's unfaithfulness to the promises (God's *logia*, see 3:2-3) has led her to reject and even crucify God's own Son - an event in which God's righteousness has been displayed. It is not to be thought that Paul *now*, as a Christian believer, is being judged in connection with that event. *He is speaking for Israel.*

Third, Paul has widely used the present tense (albeit apart from the first-person) to refer to "all" in a situation which he does not believe obtains for new covenant believers. For example, in 3:9, 20, he categorically expresses the thought that "all" are "under Sin." This "all," however, while still obtaining for those outside of Christ (who thus still belong to the "present evil age," cf. Galatians 1:4), most emphatically does not obtain for those in Christ, as becomes clear in Paul's subsequent discussion. The one who has died with Christ has been freed from Sin (Romans 6:7, 22); indeed, he is "dead to Sin and living toward God in Christ Jesus" (6:11). Sin no longer has lordship, because the believer is no longer under the old *aeon* of Torah, but the new reign of grace (6:14). Thus, the new covenant believer is no more under Sin than he is under Torah. All of this means that one must be very cautious regarding the conclusions drawn from Paul's use of the present tense. Grammar simply will not decide the question; context and content are the determining factors.

As for the juxtaposition in 7:25, it must be said that Paul's exclamation articulates a salvation-historical longing for the turn of the ages which has now been disclosed in Christ. We must ignore the chapter break and notice that the very next verse (8:1), which begins the exposition of God's solution to the plight expressed in 7:25, opens with an emphatic "now!" Whereas 7:7-25 elucidates what Torah was unable to do, Paul here goes on to describe that precisely what Torah was unable to do, God Himself *has now done* in the cross and by the Spirit (8:3).

We have already, it is clear, been providing solid reasons, not merely for questioning the arguments for the traditional position, but also, more positively, for adopting an alternative position. This position may be stated thus: *In 7:7-25, Paul speaks on behalf of Israel concerning her life under Sin and under Torah.* This passage is an interior view of the salvation-historical problem which he has been bringing up throughout the letter (e.g. 3:9, 20; 5:12-21). I will simply summarize what I believe to be very compelling reasons for understanding the passage in this fashion.

In 7:1-6, as we have seen earlier, Paul has spoken of the means by which Israel has moved out from under Torah to new life in Christ and the Spirit. He brings this argument to a climax in 7:5-6: "For when we were in the flesh, the passions of Sin, through Torah, were working in our members, bearing fruit to death; but now we have been discharged from Torah, having died by that[66] to which we were held fast, so that we serve in the newness of the Spirit, and not in the oldness of the letter."

These two verses explicitly describe *consecutive* situations, not *concurrent* ones: "*when we were* in the flesh" and under Torah, and "*now*" that we have been discharged. This statement is the last one Paul makes before entering upon the passage before us. Moreover, 7:7 opens, "What *therefore* shall we say?" Beyond question, 7:5-6 are connected to what follows. My thesis is simple: *Romans 7:7-25 is an exposition of the struggle summarized in 7:5, and 8:1-30 is an exposition of the resolution summarized in 7:6.*

This thesis is not difficult to track. In 7:5, the key elements of the situation are (1) life *"in the flesh;"* (2) *Torah provoking the passions of the members;* (3) *bearing fruit for death.* In 7:6, the key elements of the situation are (1) *release from Torah*; (2) *death by that which held us;* (3) *new service in the Holy Spirit.*

What elements do we find in 7:7-25?

---

[66] Paul writes, *apothanontes en hō kateichometha.* As in Galatians 2:20, it is Torah itself which provides the means for release from itself, namely, through the sentence of death measured against Christ.

(1) Life is in the flesh: "For we know that Torah is spiritual, but I am of flesh, having been sold under Sin" (7:14; cf. 7:18). By contrast, in 8:9, Paul writes that believers are *not* in the flesh.

(2) Torah is provoking the passions of the members: "But Sin, taking opportunity through the commandment worked in me every lust" (7:8; cf. 7:23). By contrast, Paul is able to say in 8:13 that "if by the Spirit you put to death the deeds of the body, you will live."

(3) The outcome of the struggle in 7:7-25 is the bearing of fruit for death: "but with the coming of the commandment, Sin came to life, but I died" (7:9-10). "For Sin, taking opportunity through the commandment, deceived me and through it killed [me]" (7:11). "Through the good [Torah], death worked in me" (7:13; cf. 7:24). By contrast, in 8:6, "the mindset of the Spirit is *life* and peace."

What of the elements of 7:6? Are these to be found anywhere in 7:7-25?

(1) There is no release from Torah; to the contrary, the passage throughout presupposes that the "I" is under Torah. "Now I lived once without Torah, but with the coming of the commandment, Sin came to life" (7:9). *Nomos* appears in 7:7, 8, 9, 12, 14, 16, 21, 22, 23, 25.

(2) There is no death to Torah through Torah in 7:7-25; this rather occurs in 8:2-4, where Torah's "righteous sentence" (*dikaiôma*) is fulfilled in connection with Christ's sin offering, and the Spirit employs Torah to discharge the believer from "the Torah of sin and death."[67]

(3) There is no new service in the Holy Spirit in 7:7-25; in fact, *Pneuma* drops entirely out of view between 7:6 and 8:2.[68] If 7:7-25 intends to convey the Christian struggle, this is an odd phenomenon indeed, since Paul's entire view of the Christian life is squarely pneumatological (Spirit-driven). By contrast, after the emphatic salvation-historical *now* of 8:1, the Spirit is immediately omnipresent in Paul's exposition (8.2, 4, 5, 6, 9, 10, 11, 13, 14, 15, 16, 23, 26, 27), just as *nomos* is everywhere in 7.7-25. It is the Torah in the hands of the Spirit of life who has set us free from the "Torah of sin and of death" (8:2); believers walk, not "according to the flesh" but "according to the Spirit" (8:4). In short: 7:6 finds exposition in 8:1ff., but 7:5 summarizes 7:7-25.

It thus would appear to be clear that in its entirety, 7:7-25 is an exposition of 7:5. The defining features of 7:5 appear in both subsections of this passage, 7:7-13 and 7:14-25. Thus neither in whole nor in part can the passage be referred to the present Christian life.

---

[67] For an explanation of this, see below.

[68] The observation that 7:14 identifies Torah as "spiritual" by no means undercuts this fact. For the question was never the *source* of Torah (which is God-given); the question has to do with *what Torah becomes in the hands of Sin and flesh*. It is precisely the condemnation of Sin in the flesh and the granting of the resurrection Spirit of life that is at issue, neither of which are resolved by Torah's spiritual character.

Without going into a full-blown exegesis of the passage, we may note several further features which bolster our reading.

(1) In 6:17, Paul has written that believers were once slaves of Sin, but the "I" in 7:14 is "sold under Sin."[69]

(2) In 7:9-10, Paul mentions "the coming of the commandment," which was the occasion of his death. Murray takes this to refer to some sort of "coming alive" of the commandment in the conscience.[70] But this does not appear to do justice to the objective and one-time character of the language.[71] Such language is most naturally understood as the giving of the Mosaic law at Sinai. In fact, 7:8-10 bears an uncanny resemblance to both references to Sinai which Paul has made in chapter five. In 5:13, Paul writes that "until Torah, Sin was in the world, but Sin is not reckoned to an account [Greek *ellogeitai*] apart from Torah." In other words, Sin's dominion finds it full realization and reckoning under Torah (cf. 3:20), which is why Paul can speak of dying at its coming. Note that both 7:8 and 5:13 speak of a time apart from or "without" Torah, when Sin's power lies dead (cf. 1 Corinthians 15:56: "the strength of Sin is Torah").[72]

Even more striking is the link between 7:9-10 and 5:20-21. "Now Torah *entered*, so that the trespass might abound." The result was that where Torah had entered, "Sin reigned in death" (5:21). This is precisely what 7:9-10 describes as the result of the coming of the commandment: Sin increased and brought forth the fruit of death (see also 7:13).[73]

---

[69] Interestingly, Calvin appears to take 7:14 to refer to unregenerate man ("man by nature"), going on to interpret 7:15 as referring to "a man already regenerated." ("Commentaries on the Epistle to the Romans," p. 261). This resolves the problem with 7:14, but undercuts the overall position, since 7:14-25 is generally recognized to be a unity (note the use of past tense in 7:7-13 and present throughout 7:14-25).

[70] John Murray, *Romans* pp. 250-1.

[71] Paul employs an aorist participle.

[72] This does not mean that apart from Torah, there was universal genuine spiritual life. But the experiential knowledge of Sin's power can only be known through the commandment: by Torah is the knowledge of Sin (3:20). Men were universal partakers of Adam's Sin and death, without themselves transgressing in like fashion (5:12, 14). It is only under Torah that men could once again sin "like" Adam, that is, against an objective, divinely-revealed commandment. Thus, Sin's genuine power is only known under Torah.

[73] This observation deals with a further argument sometimes made in favor of the traditional reading: the switch in 7:14 to the present tense indicates that Paul has moved from speaking of past experience (7:7-13) to his present experience (7:14-25). If 7:9, however, is referring to Sinai, it is clear that the "I" cannot refer to Paul! The shift in tense is perhaps explained most simply by Sanders, who suggests it is due to the present tense observation that "Torah is spiritual" (see *Paul, the Law, and the Jewish People*, p. 89, n. 30). Or we may simply distinguish between the arrival of the law, and the ongoing struggle under it. In any case, 7:7-13 and 7:14-25 cannot refer to different eras, whether cosmic or individual, for the defining features of both are the same. They are indeed subsections with different accents, but not different realities. The former more strongly stresses the *power* of Sin; the latter, the *frustrating character* of living with its power. Neither section refers to serving "in the newness of the Spirit" (7:6).

(3) There is a striking parallel between Romans 7 and Galatians 3:19-25. In both Romans 6.1-7:6 and Galatians 3, Paul has been speaking of the temporary character of Torah's hegemony, and Israel's liberation from it. It is thus not surprising that the issue of Torah's purpose, and indeed its *goodness*, arises. In Galatians, Paul must defend Torah against the possible charge that it is perhaps "against the promises" (Galatians 3:21); likewise, Romans 7:7-25 opens with the question of verse 7: "What therefore shall we say? 'Torah is Sin?'" In both contexts, Paul denies the negative thought; Torah is not against the promises; neither is it Sin. Both explanations, however, go on to show that it is the instrument by which God imprisoned Israel under Sin (Galatians 3:22; e.g. Romans 7:14). Galatians is explicit that the period in question was both temporary and past;[74] the parallel pushes us to affirm the same regarding Romans 7.

Romans 7:7-25, then, is not a description of "the normal Christian life."[75] Paul speaks for Israel under Torah and the dominion of Sin, not for the believer under grace and the dominion of the Spirit (cf. 6:14). The delight in God's law (7:22) is not at all problematic, for old covenant believers did indeed have this delight (Psalm 119!).

We must not miss the forest for the trees at this point. Our purpose here has not merely been to deconstruct a traditional reading, but to aid us in understanding Paul's argument. The apostle's point in Romans 7:7-25 (as in Galatians 3:19-25) is simultaneously to defend the goodness and God-givenness of Torah, while demonstrating clearly its inadequacy to deal with the problem of Sin. Torah is good, but it becomes an instrument in the hands of the power of Sin through the weakness of the flesh. Hence, "the Torah of God" which the "I" sets itself upon serving becomes "the Torah of Sin" when it articulates itself in the flesh (7.25). The "knowledge of Sin" - the intimate acquaintance with its death-dealing power - derives from Torah (3:20).

Torah is not at fault - but neither is it capable of doing more than "imprisoning all under Sin" (cf. Galatians 3:22). As we learn in what follows in Romans 8:2-4, there is only one flesh concerning which the Torah of God will not be transformed into the Torah of Sin.

---

[74] Note the "until" (*achri*) in 3:19, the "untos" (*eis*) in 3:23, 24, and the "no longer" (*ouketi*) in 3:25. The imprisonment under Sin through Torah is over.

[75] The foregoing is not intended as an assertion that pastoral application cannot employ some sort of analogy with the Christian life, an analogy based upon the fact that we are not yet resurrected, and thus our redemption is as yet incomplete (cf. Romans 8:23-5). Such application, however, ought to be cautious, not minimizing the differences between the experience under Sin and that of the new covenant believer empowered by the Spirit of Pentecost and united to the resurrected Christ.

This is the flesh of Jesus Christ; it is in administering Torah's judgment upon *this* flesh that - this one time - Torah becomes "the Torah of the Spirit of life in Christ Jesus." In this act of judgment, Torah becomes the very means of release from itself (cf. Galatians 2:19; Romans 7:6), as in the hands of the Spirit Torah releases "you" from the "Torah of Sin and death." The life toward which Torah pointed (cf. 7:10) is only realized when in its supreme act of judgment it discharges men from under its own hegemony. The age of flesh has given way to the age of the Spirit.

Sin, Judgment, and Torah

We have already seen indications that for Paul the impossibility of justification through Torah, and the inappropriateness of living under Torah, are not neatly divided issues, as (often) in later theology. His doctrine of mutual exclusiveness leads him to speak directly of justification in a context where the pressure was not in fact "theological," but had to do with simple adoption of the customs of Torah (Galatians 2:16 in context). It is thus important for us to explore how this fits together in Paul's mind.

As we have just seen, Paul correlates Torah with the sphere of Sin's domain. Sin takes its opportunity through the commandment to work death. Paul likewise correlates Torah to the sphere of divine judgment, a point which is implicit in our reading of Romans 8:2-4 just given.

In Romans 3:20, Paul writes, "from works of Torah no flesh shall be justified before Him, for through Torah is the knowledge of Sin." The first part of this verse is a reworking of Psalm 143:2, and is stated identically in Galatians 2:16. (The second part of the verse is recognizable as a restatement of Galatians 3:19, 22: Torah was introduced in order to imprison under Sin.) Comparison between the original psalm alluded to, and Paul's reworking of the text, reveals a great deal concerning both his view of salvation history and his view of the law. David had written, "Do not *enter into judgment* with Your servant, because *no one living* shall be justified before You."

Two features emerge in Paul's reworking. Beginning in the latter clause, where the allusion is most explicit, Paul has altered "no one living" to read "no flesh." This does not change the meaning of the statement, but it does reflect the apostle's eschatological understanding. For him, the *aeon* prior to Christ is the age of Sin and death (see Romans 5:12-21), and all those under it are "flesh." He deems it inappropriate to describe such people as "living;" they are "flesh," with all its connotations of mortality, weakness, and bondage.

Second, Paul has glossed God's "entering into judgment" with His servant with the phrase "from works of Torah." Thus, Paul regards the law as a means by which God enters court with men. This judgment is problematic, precisely because works of Torah do not provide ground for justification. Rather than providing flesh vindication in God's judgment, Torah discloses the knowledge of Sin.

With these two adjustments, Paul simultaneously retains the original meaning of the psalmist and indicates the fundamental problem with Torah and those under it. Torah exposes the domain of Sin (cf. 7:7-25); those who are under it are mere "flesh" and cannot enter God's judgment.

Yet in the context of Psalm 143, David is appealing to God for justification over against his enemies. This implies an acute difficulty: David the believer requires God's justice; David as flesh cannot find vindication within Torah, the place where God enters judgment with His people. Therefore, there must be an avenue of judgment, a place of vindication, outside Torah.

That is precisely what Paul goes on to expound in Romans 3:21-6: David's dilemma has been met by the righteousness of God apart from Torah, through the faith (or faithfulness) of Jesus Christ. This righteousness is only "now" (Greek *nuni*) revealed, although the law and the prophets had borne witness to it (3:21). And for all its newness, this saving righteousness does point backward as well as forward: sins which God had "passed over" are dealt with in the propitiating death of Jesus (3:25-6).

As we have seen earlier, "flesh" has been judged in Christ's flesh, but subsequent to that condemnation is vindication in the Spirit. Old creation under judgment has given way to new creation. Therefore, where Torah was weak through "flesh" under Sin, God in His righteousness has condemned Sin in the flesh through the judgment of His Son (8:3). In this way, those who were under judgment as members of the old creation are joined to Christ in His Sin-condemning death and life-giving resurrection (6:1ff.): the place of justice, of justification, outside of Torah is now complete, through Christ's fulfillment of the full measure of Torah's righteous sentence (*dikaiôma*) against Sin (8:4). Those who are in Christ have entered into God's judgment and overcome, because both His condemnation in death, and His justification in resurrection, have already become theirs (cf. 4:25; 6:3-4).

After reasserting that this eschatological gift of justification belongs to both Jew and Greek, since it is apart from Torah (3:27-30), in chapter four Paul goes on to show how faith establishes the law rather than nullifying it (3:31). The law itself (*nomos* as Scripture; cf. 3:21) has shown that justification must come apart from Torah and its works. Indeed, it was Abraham's faith which God accounted as righteousness (4:3). In the face of the weakness and death of "flesh," one's only recourse is not to works, but to God Himself, who brings life where there is none, and speaks things into existence where nothing was. This is what God counts as righteous, because it is the one response that truly gives glory to God (4:20; cf. 1:21).

For purposes of summary and clarity, then: the introduction of Torah served to provide a mechanism to deal with the sin and death which Adam had introduced. Even as Adam became a transgressor against a divine commandment (a "proto-Torah," if you will), Torah is introduced to focus transgression upon Israel, which is chosen as God's priestly nation (Exodus 19:6). Consequently, by way of Torah, transgression is "stacked up" in Israel; it is "charged to Israel's account."[76]

The "stacking up" of sin in Israel through Torah, as N. T. Wright frequently emphasizes, was for the purpose of dealing with it in Jesus Christ. In this way, God redeems the world from Adam's transgression.[77] Israel's "priestly nation" status marks her out as a sin-bearing people. When Christ comes to fulfill Israel's calling, He takes that sin upon Himself (it is charged to His account), becoming a sin-offering (Romans 8:3). As the last Adam dying under the law (where the Adamic covenant is renewed), He dies to Sin ("once for all") and thereby puts the old *aeon* of Sin to death (Romans 6:10).

It may be seen that Torah's obsolescence was built in; it was never intended to be something permanent. This is one reason why, despite its temporary character, and its feature of holding Israel back from immediate possession of the promise, Paul can still say that Torah is not "against the promises" (Galatians 3:21).

Israel's Boast

---

[76] It may be thought that this "stacking up" would refer only to *Israel's* sins, but such an assumption is inadequate. The Feast of Tabernacles, for example, had offerings for the seventy nations of the world (Numbers 29:12ff.). While the precise fashion in which this works out is not immediately transparent, nonetheless one necessary corollary of Israel's status as a priestly nation is her representative function with regard to the nations and their sins.

[77] "The law caused sin to be heaped up in one place, to flourish and abound in that single location.... God's purpose in and through all of this - in giving the Torah with this strange intention - was that sin might be drawn together, heaped up, not just in Israel in general, but *upon Israel's true representative, the Messiah*, in order that it might there be dealt with, be condemned, once and for all" (Wright, *Romans*, pp. 578-9).

We may now touch upon the theme of "boasting"[78] which runs through Romans. In addressing the Jew, Paul identifies him as one who relies on Torah and boasts in God (Romans 2:17); indeed, as one who boasts in Torah (2:23). The association here suggests that Israel's boast is based upon a notion that she will be vindicated in God's judgment, and this vindication is precisely in terms of Torah.

Paul is probably alluding here to Jeremiah 9:23-6. Those who boast should not boast in wisdom, might or riches, but in their knowledge of Yahweh. It is Yahweh who practices covenant faithfulness, justice and righteousness, and punishes those who are merely circumcised in flesh rather than heart. Paul goes on to observe that those who transgress Torah are accounted as uncircumcised; implicitly, the ground of boasting is removed (Romans 2:25-9).

As we have seen, Paul goes on in more direct fashion to undercut boasting in Torah, by demonstrating that no flesh can be justified in the context of the law. Rather, Torah exposes Israel's captivity under the domain of Sin (Romans 3:20). Thus, the only way to vindication is by means of a judgment apart from Torah, which has been displayed in God's own faithful action in Jesus Christ (3:21-6).

The plight of flesh under Sin and the demonstration of God's own righteousness in Christ, then, both exclude "the boast" (3:27). Even Abraham could not boast in works (4:2), as if he could put God in his debt (cf. 4:4). He was "dead" (4:19), and had to put his faith in God as One who gives life to the dead, and calls that into being which does not exist (4:17).

This exclusion of boasting initially appears generalized, but it must be understood in the twofold context of (1) boasting in Torah (2:17, 23); hence, the article in 3:27: "the boast;" and (2) boasting by men who are flesh (cf. 3:20). What is excluded is flesh coming into judgment with God in terms of Torah and being confident of vindication on that basis.

As it turns out, Paul's exclusion of boasting in judgment is not in fact absolute. Once the key elements of flesh and Torah are removed, there is a new ground for confidence in judgment. As Paul goes on to say, justification through Christ grants a new situation, in which *"we boast*[79] upon the hope of the glory of God" (5:2). Whereas all flesh has sinned and fallen short of this glory (3:23) and thus has had boasting excluded (3:27), here boasting in the hope of this glory is regained (cf. 5:3, 11). Paul can even go on to say that he possesses a boast in Christ Jesus in connection

[78] Greek *kauchaomai* (verb), *kauchêma* (noun: "object of boasting"), *kauchêsis* ("a boast").
[79] Greek *kauchômetha*. Translations frequently lose the link by translating this as "rejoice."

with the things in which he has labored for God (15:17). He has confidence that both his person and his works are accepted in God's judgment.

What underlies this reversal? The answer is to be found in those words of 15:17, "in Christ Jesus." Behind this is the cosmic event of Christ's death and resurrection, which we explored earlier. In Christ's death, God has condemned Sin in the flesh (8:3), and by His Spirit He has raised Christ up out of flesh into the new creation (4:25; 6:4, 9-10). Thus the place of God's judgment has shifted from Torah to Christ's flesh, and those united to Christ are therefore no longer in the flesh but in the Spirit (8:9). The result is that "boasting" (confidence in God's judgment) is now possible, outside the realm of both Torah and flesh.

Once again, the glorious words of Isaiah stand behind Paul's exposition of the gospel in Romans. Yahweh proclaims that the confession of every tongue concerning Him will be: "Righteousness and glory belong to Him, and all those separating themselves shall be ashamed. From the Lord all the seed of the sons of Israel shall be justified, and in Him they shall be glorified" (Isaiah 45:24-5 LXX). Let anyone who boasts, boast in the Lord, who demonstrates His own saving righteousness (cf. Jeremiah 9:24; 1 Corinthians 1:30-31).

The heart of Paul's polemic against unbelieving Israel, then, is to be found in his view of salvation history. Those who wish to hang onto Torah after the coming of Christ are missing the point of Torah itself, for He is its goal (*telos*, Romans 10:4). Their boast in Torah is misplaced and misguided. Israel's rejection of the Messiah in favor of maintaining Torah is a rejection of God's saving righteousness which He had long promised through the law and the prophets. Torah was a place of weakness, a place where God was preparing for the propitiation and new creation He would provide through Christ, by "storing up" transgression and shutting up all things under Sin. The resolution of the issues of Sin and judgment, which Israel seeks in Torah, can only be found in Christ.

Justification, Torah, and the Abrahamic Covenant

Sundry aspects of the foregoing analysis raise the question of how Paul understands the issue of justification during the period of the law. Why may David not enter into God's judgment through Torah? Is the problem that Torah requires "merit" which David lacks?

Certainly, David's plea indicates that he does not have the righteousness necessary to sustain such a judgment. Thus our analysis must account for that. Such an accounting has taken various forms. It is frequently asserted that Paul sees Torah as a system by which God presented Israel with the hypothetical possibility of being judged upon the basis of merit. (In recent Reformed theology, this is sometimes viewed as a "republication of the covenant of works" which was reputedly given originally to Adam as a means to merit life with God.)[80]

This, we are told, is why Paul places his own gospel in stark contrast to the "Do this and live!" of the law (Leviticus 18:5; see Romans 10:5 and Galatians 3:12). Whereas the law offered life on the basis of deeds, Paul's gospel offers life by way of mere faith. (This construct can get very complicated; a recent version is that this offer was not merely hypothetical, but meant that Israel needed to merit continued possession of the land of Israel - but not justification - through good works.)

While this is an attractively simple solution in some respects, particularly with regard to the texts in Romans 10:5 and Galatians 3:12 when taken by themselves, certain problems arise. From an evangelical viewpoint (which presupposes the integrity of Scripture), most devastating is the fact that careful study of the Pentateuch shows that if Paul is claiming that the law offers justification on the basis of merit, he has misunderstood the law. Throughout the Mosaic books, it is stressed that God is giving the land to Israel as a grant, and indeed specifically denies that they are entering into Canaan because of their own righteousness (see e.g. Deuteronomy 9:4-6). This already places the view mentioned in the awkward position of

---

[80] The older Reformed view of the covenant of works rarely tied it to merit (see e.g. Ward, *God and Adam*, pp. 116-25); I regard the later developments as unfortunate. In what follows, I am not intending to deny a parallel between the Adamic commandment and the Sinaitic Torah - a parallel I strongly affirm. I am here merely cautioning us concerning the nature of this construal.

claiming that *initial possession* of the land was by grace, but *maintenance by merit* ("covenantal nomism" with a vengeance!).

The problem, however, is more acute still. For Leviticus 18:5 does not say that if the nation as a whole keeps these commandments, it will remain in the land; it says that "*if a man* does" Yahweh's statutes and judgments, "*he* shall live by them" (or, probably better, "*in* them"). This means that the proffered blessing has to do with individuals as well as the nation as a whole, and this makes the "remaining in the land" theory rather tenuous.[81]

But going beyond even this, we must recall that Yahweh's "statutes and judgments" contextually included *means of forgiveness* (assuming repentance), and indeed Leviticus 18 itself comes at the end of a long string of chapters devoted to explaining how Israel is to seek atonement. It therefore seems rather arbitrary to suggest that the "statutes and judgments" refer strictly to the so-called "moral law," which in turn cannot be kept perfectly. One could indeed say that these means of atonement are now inoperative because they pointed forward to Christ (as noted above), and so in effect, after the coming of Christ, Leviticus 18:5 does indeed now throw one upon his own merits. But this once again makes the development of redemptive history the heart of the issue.

Romans 10:5-8

We must ask further if the popular solution is workable *from within Paul himself*. We cannot ignore the fact that in Romans 10, after citing Leviticus 18:5, Paul immediately appeals to Deuteronomy 30 in order to describe the righteousness of faith. Yet Deuteronomy 30 is as much about Torah as is Leviticus 18! Indeed, in verse 10, Moses says that if Israel obeys the voice of Yahweh, "to keep His commandments and His statutes which are written in this Book of the Law," and turns to Yahweh their God with all their heart and soul, He will rejoice over them for good as He rejoiced over the patriarchs. *And it is the very next verse with which Paul begins his citation.*

Deuteronomy 30:11-20 reads:

> For *this commandment* which I command you today is not too mysterious for you, nor is it far off. It is not in heaven, that you should say, "Who will ascend into heaven for us and bring it to us, that we may hear it and *do it*?" Nor is it beyond the sea, that you should say, "Who will go over

---

[81] This is not to deny that if Israel as a whole became collectively unfaithful, she would be spewed from the land, which is evident both from the law itself (e.g. Deuteronomy 28:64-8) and the historical texts (e.g. 2 Kings 17:6-23; 2 Chronicles 36:11-21). My point, however, is that such an understanding may not undermine two points: (1) Israel's possession of the land was by grace; and (2) the statutes and judgments were first of all significant at an individual level.

the sea for us and bring it to us, that we may hear it and *do it*?" But the word is very near you, in your mouth and in your heart, that you may *do it*. See, I have set before you today life and good, death and evil, in that I command you today to love the LORD your God, to walk in His ways, and *to keep His commandments, His statutes, and His judgments, that you may live* and multiply; and the LORD your God will bless you in the land which you go to possess. But if your heart turns away so that you do not hear, and are drawn away, and worship other gods and serve them, I announce to you today that you shall surely perish; you shall not prolong your days in the land which you cross over the Jordan to go in and possess. I call heaven and earth as witnesses today against you, that I have set before you life and death, blessing and cursing; therefore choose life, that both you and your descendants may live; that you may love the LORD your God, that you may obey His voice, and that you may cling to Him, for He is your life and the length of your days; and that you may dwell in the land which the LORD swore to your fathers, to Abraham, Isaac, and Jacob, to give them. (NKJV; emphasis mine)

In brief, it appears that the passage in Deuteronomy which Paul apparently opposes to Leviticus 18:5 could have been just as suitably chosen for the purpose of illustrating the law's principle of "Do this and live." Indeed, the very verse cited by Paul in Romans 10:6 ends with: "that you may *do* it" (i.e. this commandment!).

That leaves us with a few options. We might suggest: (1) Paul is wresting Leviticus 18 out of context; (2) Paul is wresting Deuteronomy 30 out of context; or (3) we have misunderstood Paul.

I for one prefer the last option. As we have already seen, Leviticus in context cannot mean a merit-program. This vindicates Paul's usage of Deuteronomy 30, on that level, at least. But it leaves us with the question of Paul's intention in juxtaposing these two verses.[82]

One of the first things we must observe is that outside of Paul's polemical contexts concerning Torah, he himself can say things remarkably similar to what is articulated in Leviticus 18 and Deuteronomy 30. In fact, in Ephesians 6:1-3, he appeals directly to the Decalogue's promise that it will go well with those who honor father and mother, and they will live long upon the earth.

Even more pertinently, in Romans itself *Paul makes the connection between "doing" and "life" which marks Leviticus 18:5.* In 8:13, he writes, "For if you live according to the flesh, you will die; but if by the Spirit you *put to death* the deeds of the body, you will *live*." Given the overall context of Romans 5-8, it can scarcely be doubted that the theme

---

[82] On Paul's juxtaposition of Leviticus 18:5 and Habakkuk 2:4 in Galatians 3:11-2, see below.

of "living" here stands squarely within the thought of 6:23: "For the wages of Sin is death, but the gift of God is eternal *life* in Christ Jesus our Lord." Such eternal life is the goal of God's liberation of the believer from Sin, and the ensuing "fruit unto holiness" (6:22). Paul thus has no difficulty in speaking of eternal life *wholly as a gift* (6:23), and simultaneously making a connection between the activity of the believer and that life (6:22; 8:13).[83]

If Leviticus 18 is a text advocating merit theology, it would seem that so are Ephesians 6 and Romans 8:13. Since that, however, appears to be unlikely, we must understand Paul's usage of Leviticus 18:5 in another way.

What must be underscored is that in Romans 10:5, Paul has written in the very previous verse that Christ was Torah's goal for righteousness. If that is so, it hardly makes sense for him immediately to claim that Torah's righteousness was itself a merit theology; he would be undercutting his own typology. I suggest therefore, that we have been sidetracked. In Romans 9:30-10:4, Paul has been insisting that Israel has *missed Torah's own point.* Israel, pursuing the law of *righteousness*, has missed not only righteousness (which is what we expect) - Israel has missed *the law* (9:31).

How did they fall short? They pursued the law by the works of the law, rather than by faith. That indicates that the law always intended itself to be sought by faith.

But what does it mean that Israel pursued the law "by the works of the law"? Does it mean that they tried to keep the law as a system of merit? Perhaps they did. But Paul's own elaboration specifies the problem this way: "They stumbled at that stumbling stone" (9:32); the quotation in the next verse unmistakably identifies this stone as Christ Himself. Interestingly, Paul does not here say that Israel pursued the law by works of the law, and *therefore* stumbled over Christ.[84] The problem here is not expressly articulated as a long-standing system of merit. The problem is that Christ is despised and rejected of men, rather than seen as God's righteousness; this very rejection becomes a perversion of Torah into a "law of works." Throughout Romans, it is the unbelieving rejection of Christ which Paul treats as a "fall" (note especially 11:11-2, which

---

[83] This does not, to be sure, yet delineate for us the precise nature of that connection. It does point out, however, that the connection itself cannot be construed as legalistic, and that any construction we put upon Romans 8:13 could be just as easily put upon Leviticus 18:5.

[84] Indeed, the Majority Text manuscript tradition opens Romans 9:32b with a causal connection (Greek *gar*), which places the issue on the reverse footing. Thus the NKJV: "*For* they stumbled at that stumbling stone." The conjunction is absent in other Greek manuscripts, however.

borrows the language of the Adamic "trespass" from Romans 5 and applies it to Israel).[85]

Thus, in rejecting God's righteousness, Israel seeks to establish her own righteousness (10:1-3). It is *here* that Paul speaks of Christ being the goal of the law for righteousness to everyone who believes (or perhaps: "Christ as righteousness" is the goal of the law). Paul is not claiming that righteousness *in no sense* was ever found within the context of the law. He is saying rather that the law's righteousness was always aimed at Christ; it always pointed outside of and beyond itself. Thus when Israel rejects Christ, she rejects God's righteousness - indeed, she rejects the law's righteousness, and thus seeks to establish her own, paradoxically, in the law (as also Philippians 3:9).

I suggest, therefore, that the point of Paul's contrast in Romans 10:5-8 is not primarily between "believing" and "doing." The contrast, rather, is salvation-historical; it is between, on the one hand, living by the law *broadly speaking* (even in terms of its declarations of pardon, and not just in terms of its prescriptions considered in abstraction from grace) but considered in itself, as if it pointed nowhere beyond itself - and, on the other hand, living in terms of Torah's *telos*, Jesus Christ. "The man who does those things shall live by [or *in*] *them*." During the era of Torah, Israel necessarily related to God by way of the law. Yet Torah always had Christ as its goal: He is Himself God's righteousness. So when Israel rejects Christ, she is rejecting God's righteousness, and is left with nothing but "those things" (Torah's commandments); she must live "in *them*," and thus fall short of living in God's righteousness and His new age in Christ.

This raises the question of what Paul has in view when he speaks of "God's righteousness" in this particular context. We cannot here give an extended defense of the proper interpretation of the Greek phrase *dikaiosunê Theou*, which has been heavily debated. I will simply note that where the phrase clusters most heavily in Paul (Romans 3), he quotes and alludes to no less than five Old Testament texts (Psalm 51:4 in 3:4; Psalm 5:9 in 3:13; Isaiah 59:7-8 in 3:15-7; Psalm 36:1 in 3:18; Psalm 143:2 in 3:20) whose contexts speak of divine righteousness (see Psalm 5:8; 36:6, 10; 51:14; 143:1; Isaiah 59:16-7). Moreover, the quotation of Psalm 51 in 3:4 leads directly into Paul's mention of "the righteousness of God" in

---

[85] Compare 5:15-8, 20. These two passages are the only ones in Paul which refer to one specific *paraptôma*; his usage is otherwise plural (e.g. 4:25) or nonspecific (Galatians 6:1). See also 3:1-8, where Paul implicitly identifies Israel's "unfaithfulness" to God's *logia* (3:2, referring to His promises; cf. 1:2) with her crucifixion and rejection of His Son. (Note the parallel between 3:5 and 3:25: it is in the cross of Christ where God's righteousness is demonstrated.)

3:5; likewise, the allusion to Psalm 143 in 3:20 leads directly into his extended discussion of "the righteousness of God" which begins in 3:21. In each case, the original Old Testament context refers to God's saving activity in faithfulness to His covenant.[86] It puzzles me that so many interpreters remain insistent that Paul's usage is radically different, particularly when Paul specifically says that this "righteousness of God" has been witnessed to by the law and the prophets (Romans 3:21).[87]

In 9:27, Paul has quoted from Isaiah 10:21-2, which speaks of God's act of righteousness, administering a judgment in Israel's favor over against the nations (Assyria and other enemies; note, in particular, Isaiah 10:24-5). This is set within a Messianic context in the following chapter (Isaiah 11), which describes the just "judgment" and "righteousness" by which the shoot from Jesse's stump will judge (on behalf of) the poor (Isaiah 11:3-4). *"Righteousness* shall be the belt of his waist, and faithfulness the belt of his loins" (Isaiah 11:5).

Israel has rejected this righteousness, failing to own the Messiah as God's righteousness on her behalf. Instead, she has maintained her own authority to judge the nations by means of possession and performance of the law. More than that, she has maintained the hope that Torah observance on her part will provoke God to act on her behalf: she has foolishly sought to have God "enter into judgment with His servant" (cf. David's insightful distinction in Psalm 143:1-2, a passage alluded to by Paul in Romans 3:20). This is Paul's fundamental critique of Israel in Romans 9:30ff.

This interpretation is confirmed by how Romans 10:9 develops from 10:4-8. The saving confession is of Jesus as Lord (Yahweh, Yahweh's king) and His resurrection: it is precisely here that Yahweh's righteousness has been revealed. Thus one believes/confesses unto (Greek *eis*) righteousness/salvation (10:10). This declaration is in turn supported (*gar*) by Paul's citation in 10:11 of Isaiah 28:16: "whoever believes on Him shall not be put to shame." That is, in context, the one who believes upon Jesus as resurrected Lord will be vindicated in Yahweh's judgment against the enemies of God and Israel.[88]

---

[86] Thus, the point does not rest upon what divine righteousness *can* mean in some places in the Old Testament, but upon what it means in the biblical passages from which Paul is drawing. By contrast, Piper (*Counted Righteous in Christ*, pp. 73-5) ignores the inter-textual issues and so misreads Romans 3:21-6.

[87] This is not intended to prejudge the issue of Paul's usage in other contexts, where such passages do not loom in the background (e.g. 2 Corinthians 5:21; but note the citation of Isaiah 49:8 in 2 Corinthians 6:2), or where the phraseology differs (e.g. "righteousness from God" in Philippians 3:9).

[88] This linkage of (1) divine righteousness; (2) calling upon the name of the Lord; (3) salvation;

Paul's defense of the gospel, and his critique of Israel, therefore, has here to do particularly with the advent of Israel's hope: her Lord, her Messiah, has arrived in Jesus Christ.

It is in light of such redemptive-historical issues that we may rightly question whether E. P. Sanders's focus upon "patterns of religion" has been the most helpful way of approaching the exegesis of Paul in connection with the Israel question. In Sanders's discussion, he has highlighted the issue of "getting in and staying in" the covenant.[89] This way of formulating the issue, however, marginalizes the hope of Israel, which was manifested throughout the Second Temple period in apocalyptic writing. Israel was awaiting the revelation of God's eschatological righteousness in her Messiah. By zeroing in on "getting in and staying in," Sanders has (ironically) kept the discussion of Paul too much on the level at which he found it.[90] Even as much traditional Protestant theology has focused upon individual soteriology, so has Sanders.[91]

In this particular context, however, when Paul stands against Israel "pursuing her own righteousness," he is not dealing with a "pattern of religion." He is dealing with how Israel had misconceived her eschatology. More precisely: the tendency in first century Judaism was to suppose that the revelation of God's eschatological righteousness would come in response to faithful Torah-keeping.[92] Thus it is no surprise that Israel stumbled over this stone. For Jesus challenged Israel regarding sundry issues such as Sabbath and purity. Not only was Israel not keeping Torah all that well during Jesus' ministry; if anything, it looked to Israel's leaders that Jesus Himself was *discouraging* such Torah-keeping. Thus, Israel's zeal for Torah *was* an attempt to find righteousness through the law, not necessarily within some sort of merit framework (and certainly not in connection with "getting in"), but as a means of marking

---

and (4) not being put to shame, is familiar to the Old Testament. Note e.g. Psalm 71:1-3, which not only includes these four themes, but also identifies God as "my rock" (71:3; cf. Romans 9:32-3)! We must be careful not to isolate Paul's language from its Old Testament context.

[89] The subtitle of *Paul and Palestinian Judaism* is *A Comparison of Patterns of Religion*. On "patterns of religion" and "getting in and staying in," see especially pp. 16-20.

[90] Cf. Gathercole, *Where is Boasting?* p. 111: "The taxonomy of 'getting in' and 'staying in' itself considerably downplays eschatological judgment (and by extension the role of works in that judgment) in the pattern of Jewish soteriology."

[91] Only more radically; at least traditional theology has generally had an account of the eschatological hope in its discussions of individual soteriology.

[92] See e.g. the treatment of Philo in Per Jarle Bekken, "Paul's Use of Deut 30,12-14 in Jewish Context," pp. 198-200. Interestingly, Philo is interpreting the same text as Paul (Deuteronomy 30), but in order to demonstrate that Torah-keeping will prepare for eschatological blessing. This suggests that Paul's employment of the text may well be intended to subvert existing readings (whether Philo's or that of others).

themselves out as God's faithful people, in anticipation of His eschatological deliverance. In other words, Israel *did* expect to be justified upon the basis of the works of the law. (Here, "justification" refers to God's eschatological vindication of His people, over against the pagan world under judgment.)

This discussion indicates that "justification" has often been understood too narrowly, without reference to salvation history. The justification which concerned Israel and Paul was not narrowly individual, concerned with the struggle of the soul; it had a cosmic dimension. The charge which Paul has made against Israel is not merely that she is comprised of guilty individuals (which is true enough), but that she, along with the Gentiles, is "under Sin" (Romans 3:9). In Romans 5:12-21, Paul will go on to speak of the rule of Sin and Death, a domain which held universal sway from Adam until Christ. The law cannot deal with this reality; that is one reason why Paul says "justification" cannot come through Torah (3:20).

Yet what sort of "justification" is that? On one level, Torah *did* deal with the reality of sins, by means of the rites of atonement. But such atonement leaves Israel in the domain of Sin and Death. That is why Paul says that Torah cannot give "life" (Galatians 3:21; note the "under Sin" context in the following verse). It is also why Paul stresses that Abraham considered his body "dead" (Romans 4:20). He is underscoring that those under Sin are in death, in an old creation under judgment and requiring *resurrection*. It is no accident that in this very context the apostle goes on to speak of Christ being raised "because of our justification" (4:25). The justification with which Paul is concerned is eschatological; it is grounded in and defined by the resurrection of Christ, which is the beginning of the new creation.

The new covenant prophecies promised a day in which God would forgive the sins of Israel (Jeremiah 31:31, 34). The implication is that there is an eschatological forgiveness which must transcend what is available through the means of atonement in Torah.

Israel, as we have said, sought to mark themselves out for eschatological life by way of Torah. We must be clear where Paul's quarrel is on this point. It is not with the general position that God's people mark themselves out for eschatological deliverance by way of "good works." The Thessalonians, for example, mark themselves out for just such deliverance, by way of their love, steadfastness and faith in the face of persecution and tribulation (2 Thessalonians 1:3-12).[93] But there is

---

[93] Cf. Hebrews 6:9-12, which ties assurance of future salvation to God's justice in taking into account the present work and love of the saints.

something further involved in Paul's critique of Israel: they are dead people attempting to find life in a court where life is not to be found. Unlike David, who recognized that he was under Sin, and could not enter into judgment with God, first-century Israel was willing to do so. But the only verdict Torah can grant is a verdict that belongs to the old creation. Meaning: Death, not resurrection.

This looms behind the issue of the "righteousness of God," grounded as it is in the great Isaianic prophecies of new creation, from which Paul draws throughout Romans. This is what Paul means by "life"; it is the eschatological hope of Israel. What Paul sees clearly, but what Israel in her ignorant zeal is blind to, is that God's righteousness can be displayed only as total gift, as the power of life into the place of death. This is the significance of the radical examples of faith from which Paul draws in Romans 4. David, who had placed himself outside Torah by high-handed sin (for which no atonement is provided in the law); Abraham, who leans on God for new life when he himself is "dead" (Romans 4:19). If only Israel had eyes to see, it is this death within which she stands; the hope of Israel cannot be found in Torah, but in God who gives life to the dead.

This, then, is the justification which concerns Paul. It entails the forgiveness of sins, yes - but in the cosmic dimensions of which we have spoken earlier. God's act in Christ, in condemning sin in the flesh (Romans 8:3) and raising Christ up from the dead because of our justification (4:25): this is the justification which has never before been seen. It is the justification of God, upholding the faithfulness of His own words (*logia*, 3:2-3); it is the justification of the ungodly, for that is the state of all under Sin; but this justification, in its very condemning and justifying sequence, becomes a vindication of the ungodly as over against the domain of Sin and Death - Israel's enemy, the real source of Israel's exile and despair.

We have digressed, but the digression was necessary. We must now move back to Paul's employment of Deuteronomy 30 in Romans 10:6-8. If there were no shared typology between Torah and Paul's gospel, this appeal would be arbitrary at best, outright dishonest at worst. If Torah really were intended to be about justification by works, then Paul could hardly employ Deuteronomy 30 as he does.

The fact that he cites it so extensively and freely, however, only reflects what he has just argued: his gospel of Christ is precisely the proclamation of Torah's own goal. For all Paul's criticisms of Torah as temporary, as provoking the outbreak of transgression (Romans 5:20; Galatians 3:19), and as a "ministry of death" (2 Corinthians 3), he does not claim that the old covenant faithful were intended to live by works rather than faith. Thus Paul is able to employ Deuteronomy 30 as a proper typology for the eschatological "now." The nearness of Torah is all the more translatable into the nearness of Christ, the risen Lord who has become the embodiment of Israel's hope.

This amenability of Deuteronomy 30:11ff. to an eschatological typology is fortified by its preceding context. In Deuteronomy 30:1-10, Moses foretells that Israel will indeed fail to keep Torah, that its curses will fall upon her and she will be driven into exile (30:1-2). Yahweh Himself will regather His people (30:3-5); Yahweh Himself will "circumcise your heart and the heart of your descendants, to love Yahweh your God with all your heart and with all your soul,[94] that you may live" (30:6). God will not redeem Israel because she has kept Torah; He will redeem Israel *so that* she will again obey Him.

This context confirms our reading of Romans 9:30ff. Israel has stumbled over this very restoring righteousness which God has demonstrated in His Messiah. Israel is not to place her hope in Torah, for God Himself has acted on her behalf. The word of salvation has now been made present, so that she may call upon the name of the Lord (Deuteronomy 30:14; Romans 10:8-13).

It is true that in Deuteronomy 30, Moses goes on to speak of obedience to Torah (30:8-10); indeed, that is the original intention of the very passage Paul cites (30:11ff.). For Paul, in the Christ-event the Messiah Himself has taken the role occupied by Torah.[95] Marriage to Torah has now been transferred to marriage to Christ (Romans 7:1-6); the believer is now "in-lawed" to Christ[96] (1 Corinthians 9:21; cf. Galatians 6:2).

This transfer (Christ coming in place of Torah) only illustrates further that for Paul the principal problem with the law is not that it encourages salvation by works - such a principle would make genuine typology, as Paul employs here, virtually impossible. The principal issue is eschatological life as over against life under the old *aeon*.

Galatians 3:11, 12

Paul's other handling of Leviticus 18:5, where it is juxtaposed with Habakkuk 2:4, can be read in a similar fashion, although there are minor differences due to the structure of Paul's argument. Nonetheless, in both Romans 10 and Galatians 3, I suggest that the fundamental point centers

---

[94] Cf. Romans 2:25-9!
[95] See the section below, "Christ as Torah."
[96] Greek *ennomos Christou*.

upon a movement from the old covenant period (and thus concern with the things of the law itself) to the new (and thus concern with the eschatological fulfillment of God's righteousness accomplished in Christ and the Spirit).

For starters, we once more point out that in this very epistle, Paul himself makes a strong connection between *doing* and *life*. He writes in Galatians 6:8-9, "Because he who sows unto his flesh, from the flesh will reap corruption; but he who sows unto the Spirit, from the Spirit will reap *life everlasting.* Now as those *doing good*, let us not become disheartened, for in the proper time, we will reap if we do not give up." The apostle thus is unafraid to say for his own gospel that *the one who continues in doing good will live.* A stronger analogy to Leviticus 18:5 could scarcely be sought.

In Galatians, the contrast Paul sets forth is between faith as eschatological, on the one hand, and life in Torah as immanent and therefore temporary and pre-eschatological, on the other. It is from here, to be sure, that the prevalent "believing" versus "doing" notions usually derive, since Paul says, "but the law is not from faith, but 'the one doing them shall live in them'" (Galatians 3:12).

Paul's argument in Galatians 3, not least in 3:10-13, is very dense and requires careful examination and reflection. With regard to the citation of Habakkuk 2:4, we must note that Paul is again appealing to a text that was written during the period of the Mosaic covenant. A reading that suggests that Leviticus 18 requires salvation by works, while Habakkuk 2 calls for salvation by faith, is simply untenable. In Paul's redemptive-historical scheme, both texts fall within the same overarching period. Habakkuk himself was "under the law."

Even further, Habakkuk 2:4 and Leviticus 18:5 stand in a great deal more continuity than is often appreciated. While Habakkuk is not as close to Leviticus 18:5 as is Deuteronomy 30, the fundamental meaning is certainly not in antithesis. The word for "faith" in Habakkuk 2:4 derives from the Hebrew word *'emunah*, which means *steadfastness* or *faithfulness.* (The Greek rendering *pistis* can be read either as *faith* or as *faithfulness*; the Hebrew concepts tend to shade over into one another.)[97] How does Paul's appropriation of this text relate to its original meaning?

The little prophetic book of Habakkuk, written on an occasion when God's people are being judged by nations much more wicked than themselves, is a meditation upon the problem of evil. How to justify God,

---

[97] In fact, in Qumran, Habakkuk 2:4 was interpreted as referring to faithful Torah-observance (1 QpHab 7:10-1; 8:1-3). See Dunn, *Theology of the Apostle Paul*, pp. 373-4.

not so much because He is judging Israel (which is deserved), but because He does so by the instrumentality of those who are even worse? The overall answer is that God's righteous one must live by faith that God will ultimately vindicate Himself and His faithful people; they must remain steadfast in the face of a situation that cannot be comprehended.

Thus the faith in question in Habakkuk 2:4 has to do with the horizon; we may even say that it is *eschatological* (notice the eschatological overtones of 2:14 - the earth will be filled with the knowledge of the glory of Yahweh, even as the waters cover the sea). This fits with Paul's strange language in Galatians 3:23-4, which speaks of "the faith" coming, with Christ. Perhaps the apostle is even calling Christ Himself "the faith" (or he may be referring to the *faithfulness* of God,[98] revealed in Christ).

Paul introduces the Habakkuk quotation with the statement: "that no one is justified by [or *in*][99] the law is evident." This reading suggests again that the justification which concerns Paul is not "immanent" within Torah; its advent comes through Christ, Torah's goal as God's righteousness.[100]

Stepping back to 3:11-2, then, it appears that the most satisfactory solution to this text is that Paul is once again focusing upon the "by/in *them*" of Leviticus 18:5. He has, after all, just warned that all those who are "of the works of the law" (by which I take him to mean, all those who are in the Torah covenant) are under a curse to uphold *all things* written in the book of the law (3:10). In that case, 3:11-2 is a reminder of the critical choice that is faced: life *in* the law - or life in the Christ who has been now revealed to faith.

This reading is supported, I believe, by Paul's two phrases, "of the works of the law" (Greek *ex ergôn nomou*) and "of faith" (*ek pisteôs*). If I am correct that the former refers to those who are enrolled under the Torah covenant,[101] it is natural to take the latter as covenantal membership in Christ, given the terminology of 3:23-4, which identifies Christ's advent

---

[98] The Greek word for faith, *pistis*, can be translated either "faith" or "faithfulness."

[99] The Greek word usually translated *by* is *en*; the most usual meaning of this word is locative/spatial (thus *in*). How much this locative idea enters into Paul's argument is a matter for consideration.

[100] We can look at this matter of justification and Torah in two ways: (1) people under Torah were justified (counted righteous and forgiven), but the source of their justification was God's consideration of the future coming of Christ as a propitiation for sins (see Romans 3:24-6); (2) in Christ an *eschatological* justification has arrived which was not available under the time of "flesh;" it is this great salvation-historical act which could not therefore be obtained under Torah. For more on this concept, see the section below, "The Reformation and Eschatological Justification in Paul," within the chapter, "Paul and the Reformed Tradition."

[101] See "Removal from Torah in Galatians," above.

as the coming of "faith." Since Paul can hardly mean that the subjective human disposition or activity of faith only arrived with Christ (he has, after all, just spoken of the faith of Abraham in 3:6-9), we are surely justified in seeing "faith" here as referring to Christ-as-faith.[102]

The primary accent for Paul here, then, is not, "*Do* this and live" (*doing* is bad, or even *doing* is bad if connected with *living*), but rather, "Do *this* and live" (the time of living *in Torah* is over).

That this is the correct focus is confirmed by Paul's emendation of the structure (but not the meaning) of the Leviticus text. Whereas both the Hebrew and the LXX have "if a man does/will do," Paul creates the participle, "the doing one." The result is a parallelism with the Habakkuk text which works as follows:

the righteous one	*from faith*	*shall live*	
the doing one	*these things*	*shall live*	*by/in them*

Above, the first line is Galatians 3:11 (citing Hab. 2:4); the second is 3:12 (citing Lev. 18:5). It is readily seen that this structure is apparently *intentional* - and ill-suited for placing the contrast between "doing" and "faith." The participle "the doing one" corresponds, not to "from faith," but to the substantive "the righteous one."[103] Instead, "from faith" corresponds to "these things," which refer to the commandments of Torah. The extra phrase of the second quotation, "by/in them," referring again to Torah's commandments, only doubles the effect. The contrast is not between generalized "doing" and generalized "faith," but between *Torah's commandments* and *eschatological faith* - in short, between Torah and Christ, between old covenant and new.[104]

While this reading can doubtless benefit from further nuance for the sake of clarity, it seems to me that something like it is necessary if we are to explain a number of biblical features, not least Paul's own connection between *doing* and *life* (e.g. Romans 8:13; Galatians 6:8-9). The one who

---

[102] This "faith" (*pistis*) may well refer to Christ's own faithfulness; He is the very embodiment of *pistis* who has now come. Cf. esp. Galatians 2:20: Paul lives by the faith(fulness) of the Son of God, "who loved me and gave Himself for me." On the proper translation of the Greek phrase *pistis Christou* (and related phrases), see especially Richard Hays, *The Faith of Jesus Christ*.
[103] Hays proposes that Paul understands "the righteous one" here to refer (primarily) to Christ (e.g. *Faith of Jesus Christ* pp. 134-8, 280-81). Given both the eschatological shape of Paul's argument and his views of participation in Christ, this suggestion merits careful consideration, but we cannot pursue it within the constraints of the context of this essay.
[104] Cf. James D. G. Dunn, *Theology of Paul the Apostle*: "What is in view [in Leviticus 18:5] is the way life is lived within and by the community of Israel, the covenant people. . . . keeping the law is thought of primarily as the way of living appropriate to the covenant and its continuance" (p. 152). Note also Ezekiel 20:5-26, which Dunn rightly points to as a prophetic application of Leviticus 18:5.

is within the Torah covenant must do the things of Torah; the one who is within the new covenant (that is, in Christ) must do the things of Christ: he must put to death the things of the flesh and live by the new creation Spirit.[105]

The antithesis between Paul's gospel and Leviticus 18:5 is therefore not fundamentally governed by an antithesis between grace and legalism. That antithesis certainly can be deduced from Paul, as elsewhere he makes manifestly clear that justification and life is a gift of grace which cannot be earned (Romans 4:4-8; 6:23). But while such an antithesis is necessary, it is simply not the issue which concerns Paul in connection with Leviticus 18:5. Rather, the apostle is claiming two related things: (1) It is not possible for "flesh" to bring in the new creation; that is something that only God Himself can do and has done in Christ. (2) New creation life is governed by Christ, rather than Torah, which belongs to the old creation epoch. The first of these points is a reminder that only the God who "makes the dead live and calls into being the things which do not exist" (Romans 4:17) can bring about the resurrection life of the new creation; the second is a reminder that those who participate in that resurrection life must live and walk in its terms (cf. Galatians 5:25).

The reader will have noticed that in the foregoing, I have repeatedly provided alternative ways of reading the preposition in Leviticus 18:5: "He who does them shall live *in* them," or "He who does them shall live *by* them."[106] The underlying term, both in Hebrew and in Greek,[107] may rightly be understood locatively (*in*) or instrumentally (*by*), and I have not attempted to answer definitively which is to the fore. The coordinate points of Paul's interest in the Leviticus text suggest that there is a "both/and" in view.[108] Torah is not the *instrument* of bringing about the new creation, and thus one does not arrive at life *by* works of Torah. But

---

[105] This mandate is a recapitulation of the experience of Christ, to whom the believer is united. Christ died in the flesh, and thus was raised to life by the Spirit. Since the believer participates in this reality, he is to work out that reality practically in his members. This is Paul's logic in his movement from Romans 8:1-4 to 8:5-17. He who, by virtue of being joined to the crucified and risen Christ, is no longer in the flesh but in the Spirit (8:9), must now put his mind on the things of the Spirit (i.e. the new creation) and put to death the deeds of the flesh (i.e. the old creation).

[106] So too with Paul's negative statement in Galatians 3:11: "Now *by/in* Torah no one will be justified before God."

[107] The Hebrew preposition is *bᵉ*; the Greek is *en*.

[108] It is plausible to suggest that the instrumental meaning ("by") is to the fore in Romans 10, since it is concerned with the movement from Torah to Christ, while in Galatians 3, the locative meaning ("in") is accented, since it is concerned with whether those who have already become participants in the new creation life should obey Torah. But it is doubtful we can completely empty either accent from either context.

likewise, Torah is not the *sphere* of the new creation, and thus one who is *in* Christ does not live *in* works of Torah.

Christ as Torah

As we have noticed at a number of points, Paul's Christ-Torah antithesis takes on a particular character. Christ comes, not merely to "abolish" Torah, but *in place* of it. In Romans 10:6-8, he simply glosses Deuteronomy 30's "law in the mouth" to be a confession of the resurrected Christ.

This identification of Christ "as" Torah should not be entirely surprising; as John writes, we have received from Christ's fullness, and "grace *in place of grace*, because Torah was given through Moses, while grace and truth became embodied [Greek *egeneto*] through Jesus Christ" (John 1:16-7). For John, Christ comes to fill (fill up, fulfill) Torah's role.

More importantly for Paul's purposes, since he draws heavily upon Isaiah in Romans, is the fact that there are striking similarities between Isaiah's depiction of the Servant and his depiction of Torah's future. The Servant is called to be a light to the nations (Isaiah 42:6; 49:6); likewise, Torah shall be sent forth as a light to the peoples (51:4). Moreover, like Torah, Isaiah identifies the Servant as a *covenant* (42:6; 49:8). Furthermore, whereas Isaiah prophesies that "out of Zion shall go forth Torah" (2:3), he also says that the Deliverer will come to Zion (59:20), a parallel which Paul draws tighter in Romans 11:26 by changing *to* in the quotation of Isaiah 59:20 to *from*: like Torah, the Deliverer comes forth from Zion. It is an exchange of one covenant for another, Christ for Torah; or, alternatively, Christ the New Torah.[109]

How does Paul understand this interchange? What does it indicate about Torah, and about Christ's ministry in relation to it in connection with justification?

The apostle, we have seen, has emphatically denied that "righteousness" comes through Torah (Galatians 2:21), or that one can be "justified" by it (Galatians 2:16). Yet, this would appear to be challenged by the law itself, which speaks of righteousness in connection with itself (Deuteronomy 6:25), and promises atonement through the sacrificial system (e.g. Leviticus 1:4; 4:20). Were Torah's promises of life, righteousness and forgiveness empty promises (cf. Romans 7:10)? Is Paul claiming that all those under Torah were simply cursed?

---

[109] This has a bad ring for us, perhaps, because we think of Torah primarily as "law." The point here is not that Christ is a "new set of rules," but that He is the new *covenant*, and embodies in Himself all that governs the relationship between God and His people.

No. Paul explicitly writes that God set forth Jesus as a propitiation in connection with His own forbearance in passing over previous sins (Romans 3:25). Paul's claim is not that Torah promised falsely, but that its promises are not, after all, self-referential. Sin and the curse are not finally dealt with through Torah. Torah concentrates sin, but it does not remove it. In John's words, it is "grace" (it offers a mechanism which in some way lifts the burden of sin from the shoulders of the individual). But in Paul's words, it is not "grace" (Romans 6:14: "you are not under Torah, but under grace"): "grace" is the eschatological revelation of God in Jesus Christ. (This denial of "grace" to Torah can perhaps be better understood by means of Paul's parallel statement in 2 Corinthians 3:10: "For even what was made glorious had no glory in this respect: on account of the surpassing glory." The new covenant and its attending blessing so far surpasses the old that the "glory" and "grace" of the old covenant simply come to be negated in Paul's rhetoric.)

When Christ comes in place of Torah, it is thus strength coming in the place of weakness (cf. Romans 8:3-4). The guilt of sins, merely held in abeyance through Torah, is now dealt with decisively through the propitiation in Christ's blood.[110]

These observations help us reconcile two apparently contradictory motifs in Paul's thought: that Torah was not given for the sake of righteousness (Galatians 2:21; 3:21); and that the law was "for life" (Romans 7:10), but was thwarted on account of the flesh (Romans 8:3). It is apparent from the context of Romans 8:3 that the life in view did indeed have to do with righteousness (note especially 5:17-8).

While these two thoughts are in apparent tension, one must observe that Paul is speaking from a different angle in each case. On the one hand, God did not intend for Torah itself to deal with human sin; on the other, Torah's entire mechanism was "angled" to do that - but, as Paul will later say, this is to be understood within the context of having Christ as Torah's goal (cf. Romans 10:4).

Summary: Christ and the Covenants

---

[110] It may be asked how this fits with the law's statements concerning itself, that blood rites cleansed, not only the people, but the tabernacle (e.g. Exodus 29:36-7; Leviticus 16:33). This is perhaps best answered by the enigmatic statement in Hebrews 9:23: "It was necessary that the copies of the things in the heavens should be purified with these, but the heavenly things themselves with better sacrifices than these" (ESV). The presupposition behind this puzzling verse is apparently that Torah merely effected the transfer of uncleanness from the "copy" (the earthly tabernacle) to the reality (the heavenly). God in His forbearance "passed over" sin below (Romans 3:25), but apart from Christ's sacrifice, it could not be removed from His own sight.

We have covered a great deal of territory concerning a complex subject. To see how the various strands of Paul's covenant theology hold together, it will be helpful to articulate, in summary fashion, how Christ relates to both Torah and the Abrahamic covenant.

(1) For Paul, Torah stands in the context of the Abrahamic covenant, not as the source of "life" (which would put it in competition with the Abrahamic promises), but as something alongside, under which Israel must live (see Galatians 3:15-21). This paradoxical covenantal position of Israel is reflected in Paul's reading of Psalm 143:2 (Romans 3:20; Galatians 2:16): "no flesh shall be justified" when God enters into judgment with them, and such entering into judgment occurs precisely through the works of Torah. Consequently, Israel must live under Torah, while she must simultaneously place her hope outside of Torah (implicitly, in the hope God has provided through the covenant with Abraham). Torah is God's method of entering into judgment in the sense of dealing with Sin/sin, and in that judgment His assessment is that Israel is under Sin's domain rather than His own Lordship. The implication is that Israel's history under Torah is one long record of debit accounting, one long verdict of the sentence of death. God's people are in some sense always subject to this verdict; and yet, they are forgiven. This means that the source of their forgiveness always comes from outside Torah. The legal basis for this is not evident; they simply must lean upon the promises of God (as provided in the Abrahamic covenant). This faith may rightly be described as faith in resurrection in the face of death (cf. Romans 4:16-25 and the link between death and the domain of Sin in Romans 5:12-21).

(2) The resolution of the debit account is met in God's righteousness apart from Torah, when He sets forth His own Son as the propitiation for sins, setting the account to rights, despite having for so long passed over Israel's sins in His forbearance (Romans 3:21-6). Christ exhausts the penalty due and thus fulfills its demands in His death.

(3) This act of God's righteousness is intimately related to both the Abrahamic and the Mosaic covenants, but in significantly different ways. With regard to the former, Christ is both the embodiment of the promise (Galatians 3:22) and is the ultimate promise-recipient (Galatians 3:16, 19). The release of Israel from the domain of Sin and flesh (and Torah, for that matter) becomes the means by which the promised blessing of the resurrection Spirit and the inclusion of the Gentiles in Abraham may be fulfilled. This means that He Himself becomes the "covenant to the nations" (Isaiah 42:6; 49:8), in fulfillment of the promise that the nations would be blessed in Abraham and in his seed (Genesis 12:3; 22:18). Christ thus "becomes" the Abrahamic covenant (as is implied in the *two*, rather than *three*-covenant *schema* in Galatians 4:24).

(4) Christ's relation to the Mosaic covenant is more complex. Torah's governance and judgment, however, always had Christ as its goal (Romans 10:4). It served as a child-custodian (Galatians 3:23-5) and prison guard, confining all things under the domain of Sin (Galatians 3:22; cf. Romans 3:20), with a view to Christ's coming cosmic act of redemption. By "stacking up" transgression in the priestly nation, Torah became a mechanism of condemnation upon Sin and flesh. This mechanism found its outlet when Christ came in "the likeness of sinful flesh" and God thus "condemned Sin in the flesh" in His death. In this way, the full measure of Torah's righteous sentence (*dikaiôma*) against Sin was exhausted ("fulfilled"; Romans 8:3-4). This exhaustion of Torah's penalty included the penalty against apostasy from Torah (Galatians 3:10, 13); thus Christ reconstitutes His people in Himself outside Torah (cf. Hebrews 13:10-14).

(5) Inclusion in Christ in place of Torah, however, rather than promoting antinomianism, promotes true righteousness. This is because it entails union with Christ in His victory over the domain of Sin and flesh (see especially Romans 6:14 and context), which has occurred by the condemnation of the old order in His death, and the power of the new creation in His resurrection by the Holy Spirit.

The result is that (1) God's promises of vindicating and liberating His people have been fulfilled, and thus His own righteousness and faithfulness to the covenant have been demonstrated; (2) God's people are no longer under the domain of Sin and its attendant judgment (Romans 6), but are inducted into the cosmic order of the new creation in union with their representative Head; and (3) the tension of the two-covenant situation (wherein Israel belonged both to the Abrahamic covenant and to Torah) is resolved.

Jewish Christians and a Defunct Law

If it is true that the two covenants are mutually exclusive, and that Gentiles would in fact be abandoning Christ by adopting Torah, how is it that Paul does not draw the line sharper? If Gentiles who become circumcised are defaulting from Christ (Galatians 5:2), does that not paint all Torah-observant Christians outside the circle? Is not Paul *de facto* implying that all who observe Torah's commandments are in fact outside of Christ?

This issue looms large, when we consider that Paul himself claims to "Judaize" when he is among Jews (1 Corinthians 9:20). (It is likely that this chiefly refers to his practice when visiting Jerusalem, since being Torah-observant in the context of his own Gentile mission field would presumably have forced him to act in the same fashion that earned Peter a rebuke from Paul himself.)

Even more glaring, and often treated as an inconsistency, Paul circumcised Timothy (Acts 16:1-3). Moreover, he seems to share the concern of James regarding the charge that he is teaching Jews not to be Torah-observant, since he takes the course of action which James advises (Acts 21:21ff.).

While it is not entirely easy to sort out every detail, in principle the issue is not as difficult as it first appears. There is an analogy ready to hand: in many respects, Paul treats Torah in a manner somewhat parallel to the way in which he treats idolatry (!). (Indeed, Paul moves directly from speaking of the sacrificial table of the temple to that of the table of idols in 1 Corinthians 10:18-9.)

Paul acknowledges that idols are nothing, and therefore eating food offered to idols is a matter indifferent (although, to be sure, he draws the line at eating in the idol's temple). However, if someone draws attention to the fact that the food has been offered to an idol, then Paul says to desist on account of the other person's conscience (1 Corinthians 10:25-30).

So too, on one level Paul is more than willing to argue that Torah is nothing. Indeed, in his strongest polemical work, he says that neither circumcision nor uncircumcision is anything (Galatians 5:6; 6:15). So why the vehement, anathema-pronouncing opposition (Galatians 1:8-9)? Does it all simply boil down to a "legalistic attitude," after all? No, for (among other things) that could hardly be said regarding his analogous opposition to the idolatry-related issues.

Proper understanding of the point requires getting a more secure grasp on Paul's view of the two ages, which we discussed earlier. This is in fact what underlies the parallel which we have been observing: Paul views both Torah and idolatry to belong to the old *aeon*, to the *stoicheia* of the old creation (see Galatians 4:3, 8-9).

This association of Torah with the old *aeon* cuts two ways. It means that trying to secure oneself in the people of God by adopting Torah alienates one from Christ, as we have seen throughout this study. But it also means that in fact Torah observances have no intrinsic power: "For in Christ Jesus neither circumcision nor uncircumcision avails anything, but a new creation" (Galatians 6:15 NKJV).

This perspective finds expansion in 1 Corinthians 7:17ff., where Paul advocates remaining in the state within which one was when called by Christ. This is not an absolute advocacy, to be sure, but a general principle. (A slave, for example, ought to take advantage of an opportunity for freedom offered him, 7:21.)

Thus the one who was called while circumcised is not to become uncircumcised (yes, there was a medical procedure that accomplished this for Hellenizing Jews!); nor is the one who was called while uncircumcised to become circumcised (1 Corinthians 7:18). Because, after all, these are nothing; "keeping the commandments of God is what matters" (7:19).

We find a strong hint of the ultimate grounding for this whole principle of remaining in one's original state in 7:29-31: the time is short, and the form of this world is passing away. Once again in the words of Galatians 6:15, all that matters is the new creation.

The point is that for Paul, some level of practical Torah-observance by Jews was the normal expectation - or, at the least, was acceptable to him (with the significant exception that such observance must not interfere with full integration with Gentile believers, as is clear from the confrontation with Peter in Galatians 2). They were called as Jews, and were free to continue to live as Jews. This was *not* because they were still under Torah, however, any more than eating meat sacrificed to idols (outside of the temple setting) meant the eater was a worshiper of that idol. The form of Torah-observance was simply an expression of life in this world which is passing away, and was itself a matter indifferent.

What about temple worship? Clearly the early church did gather at the temple (e.g. Acts 2:46; 3:1); and Paul did so himself, upon the advice of James (Acts 21:26). Does not the parallel with idolatry break down, since Paul disallowed eating in an idol's temple? It inevitably does, since even Paul recognized that the God of the Jews was certainly not an idol.

Nonetheless, the point remains that Paul generally adheres to the principle of remaining within one's calling. Even the apparently difficult case of Timothy falls at the edges of this. Paul circumcises Timothy as a measure to win Jews (cf. 1 Corinthians 9:20), but only because Timothy is legally a Jew, since he has a Jewish mother (Acts 16:1). (It is thus in fact no more difficult a case than all the Jerusalem Christians who were presumably circumcising their infant sons.) The men he takes into the temple for purification are Jews, not Gentiles, although the Diaspora Jews in Jerusalem at the time erroneously suppose that Paul has brought Gentiles into the temple (Acts 21:27-9).

For Paul, then, the principle of "neither Jew nor Greek" (Galatians 3:28; Colossians 3:11) means, not that everyone adopts a common lifestyle (except where it impinges upon one another), but that everything, including Torah, becomes relativized in the light of the dawn of the new *aeon*, the new creation. Jews and Greeks are free to remain Jews and Greeks, because oneness in Christ transcends these categories of the old creation. Observance of days and dietary rules are in fact indifferent (although Paul will assert that conscientious observation of such is "weakness," Romans 14:1-2, 21; 15:1). The important issue is that the new creation community lives together in a manner in which none "put a stumbling block or a cause to fall" in his brother's path (Romans 14:13), "for the kingdom of God is not food and drink, but righteousness, and peace, and joy in the Holy Spirit" (14:17).

Fulfilling the Law

I am well aware that my reading of Paul will raise protests. "If Paul really did not think Christians are under the law," it will be said, "he would not have appealed to the commandments of the Old Testament repeatedly!"

Such objections reflect the complexity of the interpreter's task, which in turn derives from the complexity of Paul's own thought concerning the law. Paul is indeed emphatic that new covenant believers are not under Torah. Yet it is equally clear that he is no antinomian (cf. Galatians 5:13). He is unapologetic that those characterized by the "works of the flesh" will not inherit the kingdom of God (Galatians 5:21). He is concerned to promote the "fruit of the Spirit," behavior "against which there is no law" (Galatians 5:22-3). There will indeed be a judgment "according to deeds," when each one will receive back in the body in correspondence to the deeds performed in that body (2 Corinthians 5:10; cf. Ephesians 6:8).[111]

It is also to be noted that while Paul insists that believers are not under the Torah covenant, they do "fulfill" the law (Romans 13:8; Galatians 5:14). "Fulfill" here in a certain sense takes on an eschatological dimension, since the matter before us is no longer simply straightforward Torah-keeping. Indeed, Paul can go so far as to say that in Christ, neither circumcision nor uncircumcision is anything, but keeping the commandments of God is what matters (1 Corinthians 7:19) - a contrast that would be completely unintelligible to a Torah-observant Jew. Thus, "keeping the commandments of God" cannot be equated with obeying the Mosaic law, and Paul's (one can only call it) casual dismissal of circumcision in this context reflects a radical reordering of what we can now call "the commandments of God."

Both the Romans 13 and Galatians 5 texts center the "fulfillment" of the law upon the commandment of love; Paul's overarching ethical

---

[111] Just how this final judgment according to deeds fits in with justification by faith alone has been the subject of a great deal of dispute. It seems to me that the simplest answer is that new covenant fruit, because it stems from the Spirit, is itself eschatological. The fruit of the Spirit cannot then be the *basis* or ground of God's final vindication (justification), since that fruit itself is an aspect of the eschatological gift. Consequently, it would seem that the relationship between the deeds and the reward is that of firstfruits and harvest. Even as the believer's works are evidence of his participation in the risen Lord, the full fruit of that participation will be given to him at the time of the final judgment. If it were otherwise, the ground of the reward would in fact be a part of the reward itself, which seems incomprehensible.

instructions and patterns indicate that this love is defined specifically in terms of Christ's self-giving upon the cross (see e.g. Philippians 2:1-11; Ephesians 4:30-5:2). This cross is the foundation of a community in which there is "one new man" (Galatians 3:28; cf. Ephesians 2:11-22), and thus the solidarity of the body of Christ without regard to the natural divisions of the old era (such as Jew-Gentile, slave-free, and male-female) becomes a defining feature of Paul's ethic. While Paul liberally lifts content from Torah (as in e.g. Ephesians 6:1-3), all of Torah is seen with new "eyeglasses," refracted through the eschatological revelation of Christ and the Spirit. (And I do mean *all* of Torah; the law-revelation as a whole is taken up into Paul's "refracted" vision.)

It may then be said, somewhat paradoxically, that Torah remains normative *Scripture*, but not a normative *covenant*, and the way in which it functions ethically is determined by God's act of redemption and new creation in Christ, with all that attends it: the climactic satisfaction of God's justice upon the cross, the gift of the Spirit, and the ingathering of the Gentiles.

It has been objected that an ethic which entails a *transformation* of the law becomes a relativistic ethic, because we will pick and choose which laws to keep, and how. Greg Bahnsen, for example, called non-theonomic[112] approaches to the law "latent antinomianism."[113] Bahnsen suggested that "the latent antinomian proceeds to arbitrate which of God's laws he deems appropriate to the Christian life today."[114]

Such claims and attendant name-calling, however, are fundamentally misleading. For first, *all* of God's laws are appropriate to the Christian life, as we have observed above. Second, even a position which wholly ignored the Mosaic law for ethical direction - which is emphatically not what we have argued for here - could not rightly be termed "antinomian," since that would still leave a huge swath of biblical ethical teaching as binding. Third, contrary to Bahnsen, our approach to Moses may be nuanced and require study (this is true as well of his own position), but the fact remains that in the terms of Paul's "fulfillment" approach to Torah, we do have divinely-inspired norms to guide us in that approach. The entirety of the New Testament is an exposition of the Hebrew Scriptures in the light of Christ. That exposition sets a binding pattern for us; we are charged with learning our Old Testament hermeneutic[115] from

[112] Theonomy, which peaked in the 1980s, suggested that the entire Mosaic law (including the civil sanctions) remains binding quite directly, unless explicitly altered by the New Testament.
[113] *Theonomy in Christian Ethics*, pp. 308-14.
[114] *Theonomy*, p. 308.
[115] I am using "hermeneutic" here to refer to the way in which we both understand the law and

the fashion in which Jesus and the apostles approached the law and the prophets.

The fact that we as Christians have widely become inexpert in the understanding of Scripture does not at all imply that there are no objective norms. It does mean, however, that the sooner we enter into comprehensive study of how the New Testament handles the norms of the Mosaic law, the sooner we will be equipped to appropriate those norms for the new covenant situation. But in the meantime, we are scarcely left without an ethic; few of us will encounter matters in daily life which are not covered by the ethical instruction of the New Testament.[116]

---

apply it to our own (new covenant) situation.

[116] Further matters related to the "fulfillment of the law" will be dealt with in the following two chapters.

Paul and Jesus

It has been beyond the purview of this essay to deal extensively with New Testament material beyond the Pauline epistles. This is not because of any supposed contradiction or disharmony between Paul and the rest of the canon, but simply a due recognition of limitations. True understanding of the New Testament writers requires getting within their conceptual and terminological worlds, and thus dealing with them individually is a much simpler (and shorter) task than attempting to correlate the many ways of saying things that different writers employ.

Nonetheless, there is a point at which we must lift our vision beyond Paul. To that end, I would like to provide a very brief angle by which I believe it would be profitable to approach the key text of Matthew 5:17-20. I draw attention to this passage, precisely because it is the strongest and most appealed-to text in terms of defending a very strong continuity between the old covenant and the new. It is thus a text which many would see as countering the reading of Paul which I have given above.

Before we can approach Matthew, however, it is necessary to summarize some of what we have learned regarding Paul's position.

One fundamental key to tying together Paul's wide-ranging statements regarding the law is simply terminological: Paul never denies that all Old Testament revelation is God-given and authoritative. Indeed, he presupposes such biblical authority everywhere. When we recognize the distinction between law as *Scripture* and law as *covenant*, we are on our way to a harmonious understanding of Paul's view of the law.

A second necessary ingredient is a recognition of Paul's view of the underlying continuity of God's purposes. While Torah as a covenant was a temporary institution, this impermanence, far from suggesting a failure in God's purposes, underscores precisely the opposite. It is because God has sent His Son and Spirit as the personal embodiment of a new covenant that Torah is no longer necessary. This guarantees that Torah's concerns do not fall to the ground, but find their true realization in Christ and the Spirit.

The movement from Torah to new covenant is thus not a surrender to evil (e.g. "I tried to make man holy through the law and that failed, so now I will just freely forgive through My Son"). The concern for holiness is at least as prominent in the new covenant as in the old (cf. the "how much more" arguments of Hebrews); and free forgiveness, likewise, was a genuine reality in the old covenant just as in the new (cf. Psalm 32:1-2). While Torah dealt with sin in a preparatory way, the coming of the Son deals with it definitively and eschatologically, rendering Sin's dominion void.[117]

With these thoughts in mind, we now approach Matthew 5:17-20. The English Standard Version renders the passage in question this way:

> Do not think that I have come to abolish the Law or the Prophets; I have not come to abolish them but to fulfill them. For truly, I say to you, until heaven and earth pass away, not an iota, not a dot, will pass from the Law until all is accomplished. Therefore whoever relaxes one of the least of these commandments and teaches others to do the same will be called least in the kingdom of heaven, but whoever does them and teaches them will be called great in the kingdom of heaven. For I tell you, unless your righteousness exceeds that of the scribes and Pharisees, you will never enter the kingdom of heaven.

These verses are frequently understood to be insisting that Christ *confirms* the law, even down to its minor details (a position taken furthest in the movement known as "theonomy," represented most rigorously by Greg Bahnsen's *Theonomy in Christian Ethics*). Even the most insignificant details of the law remain binding (unless overturned specifically by new covenant revelation).

However, this reading is problematic on several counts.

> (1) The allusion to the "jots and tittles" suggests that *no "unless" can be justified.* Jesus here is speaking of the Law and the Prophets without the slightest exception: *none* of this will be "abolished" by Him; all of it will be "fulfilled" by Him. Thus theonomy refutes itself: since no one suggests that *no change* occurs between the Testaments, "fulfill" cannot here be understood as bare confirmation.

> (2) In fact, contrary to Bahnsen and even some more mainstream Reformed commentators, "fulfill" (Greek *pleroô*) in Scripture *never* means "confirm." The terminological range centers upon the idea of "filling" or "completing," and implies "unfinished business" prior to the point of fulfillment.[118]

> (3) The reference to the *prophets* all but falls out of view in the interpretation of Bahnsen (as well as that of many other Reformed authors). The issue of abolition/fulfillment, while focusing upon so-called "ethical" issues in the immediate context of the Sermon on the

---

[117] The movement from lower-case "sin" to capitalized "Sin" here is intentional. The old covenant had little or no means of dealing with Sin, which is a cosmic salvation-historical problem.

[118] See especially Vern Poythress, *The Shadow of Christ in the Law of Moses*, Appendix C.

Mount, is simply not exhausted by them. Jesus' statement in 5:17 is programmatic for His entire earthly ministry, not simply His ethical teaching. Jesus' mention of the fulfillment of the prophets is not to be ignored or marginalized.

(4) In connection with this, a proper understanding of "fulfillment" thus requires an examination of how the term is employed elsewhere throughout Matthew's Gospel. Such study makes very clear that "fulfill" does not mean "confirm." In Matthew, Christ's fulfilling activity entails taking up the whole of God's previous (Old Testament) dealings with Israel and transforming them within His own Person and work.[119]

A proper understanding of Matthew 5:17-20 involves a recognition that the "fulfillment"of Torah and the prophets moves us beyond any upholding of the Mosaic covenant in its literal and original form. Thus the "jots and tittles" which cannot pass refer, not to the permanent validity of each of the sundry commandments of the Mosaic covenant as such, but to the thoroughgoing way in which Christ takes up the whole of the preceding revelation, both in His own life and ministry and in His teaching. The *whole* Torah (and not simply the "moral law") is *validated and established* in Christ, and the *whole* Torah (and not simply the "ceremonial law") is *transformed into something new* in Christ. None of the commandments falls to the ground (mere abolition) under the new covenant; none of the commandments is simply confirmed (mere repetition) under the new covenant. Because Christ Himself comes in the place of Torah, the whole preceding revelation is now channeled through His life and work. He has come, not to repeat, but to glorify.

Even the Decalogue is subject to this transformation, as is evident from the biblical treatment of the Fourth Commandment. No matter how high our "sabbatarianism" might be, we simply must concede that the new covenant does not countenance a seventh-day Sabbath.[120]

In this light, it can be seen that the "fulfillment" of Torah outlined in Matthew 5 conforms to Paul's own doctrine of the fulfillment of the law. Torah's fulfillment does not aim at bringing believers under the Mosaic covenant; nor, on the other hand, does it disestablish the law as authoritative Scripture. Rather, this fulfillment compels us to read Israel's Scriptures in a new way, through the lens of Christ's advent and the Spirit's work. The Scripture is *one story*, but that one story is not a simple straight line. It is an intricately woven plot, a story of complex beauty. Thus Paul's complex position on the law is faithful to the complexity of the biblical story itself.

---

[119]On this and related points, see my study, "Fulfillment in the Gospel of Matthew."
[120]Cf. Galatians 4:10; Colossians 2:16-7.

Paul and the Reformed Tradition

As confessional Christians standing within a doctrinal tradition, it is imperative that we take the further step of considering how our exegetical analysis interfaces with our tradition. Although the present study can only touch upon this issue, it is appropriate to ask such questions in connection with two issues upon which our study impinges: the so-called "moral law," and justification by faith alone.

The "Moral Law"

The Reformed tradition has a long history of identifying a "moral law" to which believers in every age are subject. How does Paul's view of the temporary character of the Mosaic covenant as a whole stand in relation to this tradition?

The first thing that we must recognize is that terminological differences between Paul and the tradition are not in themselves problematic. Indeed, there are terminological differences between Paul and his fellow New Testament authors. This is particularly true of James, who speaks in a new covenant context of the moral force of a "perfect law of liberty," in which the Christian must continue (James 1:25). It is questionable whether Paul would have employed that particular terminology. It would not follow, however, to conclude that Paul would have disagreed with James. The difference is that Paul manifestly prefers to reserve "law" terminology to refer to the Mosaic covenant (or the Scriptures from the perspective of the old covenant); James is using the term more broadly.

This insight must assist us as we approach the Reformed tradition and the questions, both of the tradition's faithfulness to Pauline teaching, and the confessional viability of our reading of Paul in relation to that tradition.

The *Heidelberg Catechism* asks, "What is the law of God"? and forthwith cites the Decalogue (Q/A 92). From this, it is immediately evident that the Catechism is not speaking univocally with Paul; for Paul, the "law" encompasses the whole of the Mosaic covenant, as marked out by circumcision, dietary laws, etc., and not simply the Decalogue. As with Paul and James, Paul and the tradition differ terminologically. But is the difference more substantial?

The problem in some people's minds is that they suppose that the Decalogue is a "timeless" moral law which has been unchanged from Adam onward, and moreover, that this understanding of the Decalogue is indeed the normative Reformed position. This position, it is thought, is bolstered from a biblical perspective by the fact that the Decalogue alone, out of the whole Mosaic revelation, was recorded by God's own finger on tablets of stone, thus testifying to the unchanging validity of the Ten Commandments.[121]

If this reading were correct, we would be forced to admit that our reading of Paul does not entirely coincide with such a view. We have suggested that Paul's handling of the *entire* Mosaic law, including the Decalogue, is understood through the lens of the Christ-event, including the sending of the Spirit, and that his viewpoint is in no way to be understood as a simple "carrying forward" of the (unchanged) law, whether in whole or in part. Moreover, for Paul, the writing of the Decalogue on tablets of stone, far from being a sign of eternal, unchanging validity, is a sign of the powerlessness of Torah as a ministry of death in an age prior to the glorious ministry of the Spirit of Pentecost (see especially 2 Corinthians 3:3, 7).

We must observe, however, that contrary to the claim we oppose, the exposition I have given of Paul above is in no way contradictory to the confessionally Reformed position on the moral law. It is true that the *Heidelberg*, for example, gives no explicit awareness of any alteration in the law from old covenant to new. And yet, its own treatment of the Decalogue assumes such a transition without argument. This is evident enough in the treatment of the Fourth Word, where there is no question of advocacy of a seventh-day Sabbath, and in fact the exposition sounds nothing like Old Testament explications of the commandment. A similar point could be made regarding the other Reformed confessions. This already shows that the Reformed tradition has always had at least an implicit sensitivity to the fact that the Decalogue does not function in the same manner for the Church as it did for old covenant Israel.[122]

---

[121] Cf. Ward, *God and Adam*, p. 194. This position is in fact already rendered problematic by the fact that the Ten Words change form between Exodus 20 and Deuteronomy 5. As James Jordan has pointed out, there is covenantal progression reflected behind this alteration, thus hinting at the "instability" of the Decalogue itself. See Jordan, "The Ten Words and Their Liturgical Usage."
[122] This analysis holds for the Westminster standards, as well. While the *Confession of Faith* calls the moral law "this law," indicating continuity between redemptive-historical periods, it does not suggest that the moral law undergoes no change. Moreover, the *Larger Catechism* explicitly articulates such change in its treatment of the Fourth Word (Q/A 116; cf. *Shorter Catechism* Q/A 59).

It is evident from Paul that the Church must adopt a position which in general amounts to the affirmation of the validity of the "moral law," as the Reformed tradition has done. For while "fulfillment of the law" by the believer is in Paul somewhat broader than the keeping of the Ten Words (in some form), it nonetheless includes that, as is testified to his sundry appeals to them in connection with exhortations to godly behavior (e.g. Romans 13:8-10).

On the other hand, this does not mean that a simple abstraction of the Decalogue from the Mosaic revelation (i.e. a neat severing of "moral" law from "ceremonial" and "civil" law, as if the former simply carries forward and the other two are abolished) is a thoroughly adequate way of dealing with the question of Christian ethics. For Paul, the *whole* Mosaic revelation is material by which the believer is "instructed in righteousness" and "equipped for every good work" (2 Timothy 3:16-17); and moreover, once again, the *whole* Mosaic revelation is subject to reconfiguration through the lens of new covenant fulfillment, including the Decalogue.

Nor may we isolate the Fourth Word on this point. We may point, for example, to the very first, most foundational, of the Ten Words. It is true that the God of the old covenant is the very same God of the new covenant. And yet, while we acknowledge that God in His nature has not changed, neither ought we pretend that old covenant Israel could have formulated the Nicene Creed. God has always been Trinity; but it is only now that we worship Him as Father, Son and Holy Spirit. Thus the very First Word is dramatically renewed and reconfigured by the Christ-event.

We could also point to the issue of continued marriage with unbelievers. Although it is unacceptable under either covenant to *marry* an unbeliever (1 Corinthians 7:39; cf. 2 Corinthians 6:14), yet it is only under the new covenant that the believer is permitted and encouraged to *remain in* an existing marriage with an unbeliever (compare 1 Corinthians 7:12-5 to Ezra 9). This alteration apparently arises out of (1) a stronger call to mission; (2) a more robust holiness in the new covenant, which tends now to spread outward rather than collapsing inward;[123] and (3) a more vital practical power in the believer's life, namely, the Spirit of Pentecost. Thus the ethical shape of the seventh commandment alters in connection with the Christ-event.

In addition to these differences on an ethical level, we need to be aware of the dangers of employing "moral law" terminology in terms of the possibility of blunting Paul's eschatological reading of the Mosaic law.

---

[123] Cf. Haggai 2:11-3.

81

The danger of the language is not simply that we fail to recognize the ethical differences between how the old covenant and the new employ the Decalogue. The more fundamental danger is that the "moral law" terminology obscures the Pauline teaching that *the old covenant Israelite sustained a different relation to the Decalogue than does the new covenant believer*, as is evident from Romans 7:1-6. Whereas in some sense the Israelite was "married" to Torah as a covenant (including the Decalogue, as is evident from Paul's own exposition of Romans 7:5 in 7:7-25), the new covenant believer has been released from that relationship. Indeed, Paul uses very strong language in this regard; the Israelite, along with all those before Christ, was "in the flesh," whereas the Christian is "in the Spirit" (see e.g. Romans 7:5-6). Thus we must be aware of the decisive eschatological transition that has occurred with the Christ-event. We may say that in some sense, the old covenant believer related to God through Torah, while the new covenant believer "relates to Torah" through Christ Himself. It is now the very Person of Christ who is "a covenant to the nations," whereas Torah was the covenant to Israel under the age of the flesh (cf. Isaiah 42:6; 49:8). Old covenant believers related to Yahweh through a child custodian (Galatians 3:23-5; 4:1-3).

By these observations, I am not suggesting that the "moral law" terminology ought to be discarded. I am simply highlighting the limitations inherent in it. While I myself generally try to avoid employing "law" terminology to refer to new covenant ethical responsibilities when possible (particularly in connection with speaking of Paul), I recognize that it remains biblical and confessionally helpful. The point, however, is that we need to supplement our "moral law" concept with (1) an understanding of the distinction between our terminology and Paul's; and (2) a recognition of the redemptive-historical issues which Paul defends so strenuously. The issue is not whether speaking of a "moral law" is wrong, but that we strive to maintain fuller biblical balance than we sometimes have done in our tradition. This will, I believe, help guard against treating the "moral law" in a fleshly way; we will be better reminded to treat the commandments as embodied expressions of life in the Spirit, rather than simply duties to observe out of "thankfulness." We are not simply Torah-keepers; we are members of the new covenant, living out of the miracle of the Christ-event and the power of the Spirit of Pentecost.

Sola Fide and Saving Faith in Paul

This essay has not been a study of Paul's doctrine of justification as such. However, as is widely recognized - and as has been very evident at various points in our exploration here - Paul's teaching on the law is integrally related to his understanding of justification. Consequently, while in this section I will not attempt to provide a full exposition of the Pauline doctrine of justification, it is appropriate to consider how our study of the narrower question of Paul and the law does impinge upon the Protestant doctrine of *sola fide* ("faith alone").

Our survey of Paul's teaching has indicated that his primary thrust is salvation-historical. In both of his epistles which deal heavily with the law (Galatians and Romans), his main point is not that we must be sure to treat the law as a rule of gratitude, rather than a means of achieving justification through merit; rather, his main concern is to show that the new salvation-historical situation necessitates a move out from under the Mosaic covenant. The alternative is Moses *or* Christ, not both/and.

It should be recognized, however, that this does not at all imply that the Protestant teaching of *sola fide* does not derive legitimately from Paul. Both in his positive expositions of the meaning of the Christ-event as over against Torah (such as in Romans 4) and in contexts unrelated to discussions of the law (e.g. Titus 3:5), Paul is clear that right standing with God is not granted to human beings upon the basis of works of righteousness which they have done.

On the other hand, this cannot be construed as an admission that every conceivable "Protestant" articulation of *sola fide*, and every deduction ever made from it, can be defended from Paul. In recent debate, for example, the question of whether justifying faith is "complex" or "simple," whether it is in some sense "active" or wholly "passive," has arisen, and many men intending to defend Reformational orthodoxy have insisted that only a completely simple and passive faith justifies, and that only this view genuinely safeguards the doctrine of *sola fide*.

By itself, this subject requires an essay on historical theology. Here I will merely set forth a few observations that I believe will assist us in further reflection.

> (1) Slogans such as "justification is by faith alone, not by a faith that is alone" were very familiar at the time of the Reformation and on into the era of "Reformed orthodoxy."[124] Such statements would certainly appear to affirm that the *faith* that justifies is an active one, because faith produces the accompanying fruits.

---

[124] E.g. Calvin, *Institutes* III.XVI.1 (p. 798): "For we dream neither of a faith devoid of good works nor of a justification that stands without them. This alone is of importance: having admitted that faith and good works must cleave together, we still lodge justification in faith, not in works. . . . we are justified not without works yet not through works." Cf. also Francis Turretin, *Institutes of Elenctic Theology*, Volume 2, 16:VIII:VI, XIII (pp. 677, 680): only faith justifies, but a solitary or "alone" faith does not.

(2) In the view of Calvin and many others, justification is a gift of union with Christ. That union conveys the "twofold benefit" of justification and sanctification.[125] On this view, union with Christ is accomplished receptively, and accomplishes both benefits. In that respect, sanctifying faith and justifying faith are *one* faith, not two.

(3) There is no hint that for Paul, faith's activity is "suspended" until justification takes place, after which faith becomes active.[126] To the contrary, in the context of the debate with the Judaizers, Paul denies that either circumcision or uncircumcision counts for anything, but "faith *working* through love" (Galatians 5:6). While this certainly does not mean that for Paul, love justifies (or contributes to justification), yet it does mean that justifying faith is an active faith which does work through love. In terms of the historic Reformed position, it is significant that the Belgic Confession explicitly makes this same connection between Galatians 5:6 and justifying faith.[127]

(4) On the biblical level, a view of the complete passivity of justifying faith does not square all that well with Paul's outline of Abraham's faith in Romans 4, which is described in very robust terms of leaning upon God's "unreasonable" promises in the face of natural impossibilities (Romans 4:17-22). Indeed, in his act of believing, Abraham is explicitly described as "giving glory to God" (Romans 4:20).

(5) If we do employ the language, then, we must be very careful with what we mean by "simple" and "passive." If we intend to say that justifying faith in its initial instrumental capacity of union with Christ Christ is *receptive* and in that sense passive, there is no problem. In this connection, we may compare the issues of Christ's active and passive obedience. Christ's passive obedience does not refer to inactivity or inertia, but to His *receptivity* to His role as sin-bearer. As has been well recognized, Christ does not have "two obediences," but one obedience which may be considered under two aspects or capacities, and these capacities may be distinguished but never separated.[128]

---

[125] Calvin, *Institutes* III.XVI.1 (p. 798): "we are justified not without works yet not through works, since in our sharing in Christ, which justifies us, sanctification is just as much included as righteousness."

[126] On the active nature of saving faith, cf. William Ames, *Marrow of Theology*, p. 242: "Faith is our life as it joins us to God. But it is also an act of life because it is a virtue and our duty towards God."

[127] "It is so far from being true that *this justifying faith* makes men remiss in a pious and holy life, that on the contrary without *it* they would never do anything out of love to God, but only out of self-love or fear of damnation. Therefore it is impossible that *this holy faith* can be unfruitful in man; for we do not speak of a vain faith, but *of such a faith which is called in Scripture a faith working through love*, which excites man to the practice of those works which God has commanded in His Word" (Article XXIV; emphasis mine).

[128] "It is our Lord's *whole work of obedience* in every phase and period that is described as active and passive. . . . The real use and purpose of the formula is to emphasize the two distinct *aspects* of our Lord's vicarious obedience" (John Murray, *Redemption Accomplished and Applied*, p.

One may add that in general, the supposed Pauline contrast between "believing" and "doing" has probably been somewhat overstated in much Protestantism. As we saw in our study of Paul's juxtaposition of Leviticus 18:5 with other Old Testament texts (Deuteronomy 30:11ff. in Romans 10:5-8, and Habakkuk 2:4 in Galatians 3:11-2), the main intent of the contrast is indeed not between believing and doing. In fact, the very text Paul cites in Romans 10:8 (Deuteronomy 30:14) ends in "that you may do it" - an observation that apparently falsifies the common assumption regarding Paul's point.

To this must be added the insight that Paul holds two things together which appear to be in tension: justification is not by works of righteousness, and yet, paradoxically, faith itself is accounted as righteousness, and is the way of justification. Paul, it is clear, sees no contradiction here, for he maintains both of these points within the same context (Romans 4).

Related to this is the fact that for Paul, as for other New Testament preachers, faith is obedience. (Please note: this is *not* the same as saying that "obedience is faith;" it is a logical fallacy to suggest that because A is B, therefore B is A.) Even as Peter proclaims that the Holy Spirit is given to those who obey Christ (Acts 5:32), so Paul says that his apostleship is "for the obedience of faith" among all nations (Romans 1:5; cf. 15:17-8; 16:26). In both instances, what is meant is that believing is the supreme response of obedience (cf. also John 6:29).[129]

Thus, it is not possible to make an absolute claim that justification is not conditioned upon righteousness or obedience *whatsoever*. The one "righteousness" which God recognizes, the one "obedience" without which there is no justification, is faith.[130]

However, this may not be used as a wedge to pry open a door for justification upon the basis of works of obedience in general. As we have seen, Paul excludes such a notion, even in contexts apparently unrelated to discussions of Torah. This exclusion reflects the unique character of justifying faith itself, as described by Paul in this very context: it is faith in the God who gives life to the dead (Romans 4:17, 19, 24-5). When this

---

21; emphasis mine).

[129] Again, William Ames: faith is "a virtue and our duty towards God" (*Marrow of Theology*, p. 242).

[130] So too Luther, *Lectures on Galatians*, pp. 226-36. Cf. John Bunyan: "faith when it hath received the Lord Jesus, it hath done that which pleaseth God; therefore, the very act of believing is the most noble in the world; believing sets the crown upon the head of grace; it sets its seal to the truth of the sufficiency of the righteousness of Christ (John, iii. 33), and giveth all the glory to God; and therefore it is a righteous act: but Christ himself is the 'Righteousness that justifieth,' Rom. iv. 20" (*Justification by an Imputed Righteousness*, p. 25).

is understood within the broader context of Romans 1-5 (particularly Paul's articulation of the realm of Sin and Death in 5:12-21), it is easy to see that the only righteousness that can avail for justification is precisely the righteousness of faith. For it is only the God who gives life in the face of death who can set right this condition.

Yet the fact that the faith which justifies is in fact obedience does indicate that justifying faith is not cut asunder from the rest of the Christian life, such that it remains passive and immobile, *sui generis*. Justifying faith is the very faith which works through love; the initial obedience of faith forms a matrix, so that that which has been begun in the obedience of faith will necessarily carry forward in the obedience of good works.[131]

The Reformation and Eschatological Justification in Paul

If there was one defining feature of the Reformation's treatment of justification, it was a sustained defense of its forensic nature. Justification, over against Rome, is to be construed as God's verdict or pronouncement of "righteous," not as a process of sanctification by which men may amass condign merit for life eternal.[132]

In our reading of Paul, we have noted that justification in Christ entails a deliverance from the domain of Sin. The question which arises is whether this "transformative" aspect of justification compromises its purely forensic character.

The answer is "No." At the outset, we must note that this transformative aspect does not refer to a process of renewal, but to the *definitive act* which occurs when the believer is united to Christ. This act is forensic.

It must be kept in mind that the biblical role of judge was somewhat broader than the roles played by modern judges. The judge was expected to *execute his sentence*; apart from this, his verdict was simply incomplete. Thus the "unjust judge" of Jesus' parable was expected to avenge the widow upon her adversary (Luke 18:1-8). This is why the book of Judges concerns, not merely decision-makers, but *deliverers*. The "justification" with which they were concerned involved a vindication of God's people, which demonstrated their status before God and condemned their enemies.

---

[131] Note especially the connection Paul makes between the "obedience from the heart" to the gospel proclamation (Romans 6:17) - given the aorist tense, an apparent reference to initial faith - and the obedience of right conduct (6:15-6, 17). Saving faith makes one a servant of righteousness.

[132] Compare e.g. *Catechism of the Catholic Church*, p. 537, which contends that justification "establishes cooperation between God's grace and man's freedom," and goes on to argue that the goal of this cooperation is that man will be able to merit eternal life.

Paul implies in numerous ways that justification under Torah was incomplete. He does so by identifying the entire salvation-historical period as "under Sin" (Romans 3:9; Galatians 3:22). Torah is the place of God's judgment; and yet, paradoxically, it is a place where no flesh shall be justified (Romans 3:20; Galatians 2:16). Thus there is no full and clearly legal basis of justification in the passing over of sins under Torah, which is why it is Christ's propitiation which spells out, and indeed fulfills God's justice (Romans 3:24-6). It is in Christ that justification fully occurs, when Sin is condemned in the flesh, and the righteous one is fully vindicated through resurrection.

This courtroom action involves three parties: (1) God, (2) the righteous one, and (3) the enemies of God and of His righteous servant. The enemy, principally, is Sin as manifested in the flesh. When God punishes Sin in the flesh in the death of His Son (Romans 8:3), He is adjudicating on behalf of the righteous, and condemning the enemy of the righteous. *This is a judicial act.* It is wholly forensic.

The raising of the righteous one, like the condemnation of the enemy, is also a judicial act (cf. Romans 4:25). It is the vindication of the righteous, over against the wicked; it is the Judge's declaration that *this* one is in the right in His courtroom. Thus the resurrection is also wholly forensic.

Yet this dual forensic act, this condemnation and vindication, is *as such a transformative event.* The judicial character of the event in no way undermines the fact that the justification in question involves a transformation, an alteration in the situation of the righteous one, Christ. The justification entails a movement from life (and death) under flesh and its domain to life in the Spirit, a transition from the old creation to the new. And this same justification which belongs to Christ is also the justification of the believer, who is united to Him. Consequently, *in justification* - in a wholly forensic event - the believer is removed definitively from the domain of Sin and is empowered by the Holy Spirit to serve in newness of life. This is the Pauline teaching on eschatological justification.

This explains why Paul can speak of being "justified [*dedikaiôtai*] from Sin" (Romans 6:7) as an explanation of the believer's deliverance from Sin's power. This usage has often wrongly been dismissed or set aside from Paul's "normal" usage, as if it had nothing to do with his view of justification. Once we understand, however, that God's eschatological justification in Christ includes vindication over against the great enemy, Sin, the difficulty is removed.[133]

---

[133] It should be noted that this aspect of justification is not over against God's justice, but over

Likewise, we can hereby understand how Paul can move so seamlessly between speaking of justification and speaking of the Holy Spirit. The Spirit, it seems, is not merely some sort of posterior evidence of justification; rather, Paul describes God's relationship to the Galatians as one that has "*begun* in the Spirit" (Galatians 3:3).[134] In Galatians 3:14, he goes on to parallel the "blessing of Abraham" upon the Gentiles with the reception of the Spirit; he has earlier identified this blessing as justification (Galatians 3:8-9).

This explains, finally, why the issues of condemnation, justification, and transformation are so thoroughly interwoven in Romans 8:1-4. Paul simply does not see himself as speaking of two different subjects (such as "justification" on the one hand, and "definitive sanctification" on the other). The release from condemnation (8:1) is understood in terms of a release from "the Torah of Sin and death" (8:2). (In the context of Romans 7:7-25, "the Torah of Sin and death" has to do, not only with Sin's *guilt*, but its *power*, its lordship.) This release has been effected through God's condemnation of Sin in the flesh (8:3). This is an achievement that Torah and its sin-offerings could not accomplish, but Christ as sin-offering has achieved for us. The carrying out of the full weight of Torah's righteous sentence (*dikaiôma*) is accomplished once-for-all (Greek aorist: *plêrôthê*), and yet in us (*en humin*): this is the initiation to, and foundation for, walking in newness of life through the Spirit of the new creation (8:4). Paul is not confusing justification and sanctification; he is explaining what God's eschatological verdict has accomplished in Christ's death and resurrection. This entire event is significant precisely in its forensic character: it is wholly concerned with *justification*.[135]

Careful reflection shows that such teaching is *not* in conflict or tension with the Reformation concern.[136] The act of transformation in question is

---

against Sin. (It is nonetheless an act *of* God's justice, on the basis of the believer's union with Christ.) Thus there is no room to speak of forgiveness being granted on the basis of renewal, as suggested by the scheme of Osiander.

[134] Compare also Acts 15:8, where Peter identifies the outpouring of the Spirit upon the Gentiles as God's "bearing witness" to them, i.e. testifying to His acceptance.

[135] It is to be noted that Turretin recognizes Romans 8:4a as a reference to justification (see e.g. *Institutes of Elenctic Theology*, Volume 2, 16:III:XXVIII, p. 656). However, he leaves the connection to 8:4b unexplored.

[136] It should be noted that some early Reformed theologians, such as Zwingli, Oecolampadius, Bucer, and Bullinger (in varying ways) also accented a transformative element in justification. On this, see e.g. Robert Letham, *The Work of Christ*, pp. 188-9; Alister McGrath, *Iustitia Dei*, pp. 219-26. The point of my discussion here is not to backtrack as far as those theologians (whose views I generally consider too subjective and moralistic), but to suggest that (1) a transformative element in justification is a Reformation concern, and that (2) the Pauline reading I have proposed preserves both that transformative insight and the objective, forensic concern of

not a means of placing the believer in a situation to amass condign merit. Nor is justification upon the *basis* of this transformation; rather the reverse, the transformation is itself the articulation of God's justifying verdict. The whole event, therefore, is significant precisely in its own forensic character as God's declaration of "righteous."

It may well indeed be hoped that by a proper understanding of Pauline teaching, there may in the long run be a basis for Rome to move to a forensic view of justification. Perhaps a new accent by Protestants on "justification as transformation" will help facilitate such a move. We ought to welcome that; it should not be our goal to disqualify Rome from the truth, no matter what she does, as if the goal of orthodoxy were a constantly-receding line on the horizon.

But in the meantime, we may and must say clearly that justification is God's verdict of "righteous," and that Rome's notions that justification is a process, and that God's verdict is at best partial in the present, are serious errors. In Christ's death and resurrection, the full weight of God's judgment against Sin has been borne, the full weight of God's favor for His righteous ones has been declared, and those in Christ are full participants in that liberating verdict.

---

later Reformed thought, in a way which does not undercut *sola fide*.

Conclusion

Paul's analysis of the law arises within the context of polemical confrontation on two distinct but related fronts: ostensibly-Christian Judaizers, and unbelieving Israel. The apostle's point of concern in both these conflicts is focused upon Israel's law - Torah. Paul's position regarding Torah is determined by the eschatological revelation of Israel's Messiah, who as the climax of Israel's history and her promises, represents a self-contained covenant which will allow for no competition.

Not that Torah served no good purpose. Among other functions, it served to focus transgression in Israel, to the end that Christ might bear it as the Last Adam. As a result, Torah has now exhausted its redemptive-historical calling; it has reached its goal in Christ. Christ's sin-bearing is simultaneously the liberation of Israel from the yoke of Torah, so that she might be released to live in the new age of the Spirit and receive the Gentiles into full communion in fulfillment of the promise to Abraham.

Consequently, there can be no question of allowing Gentiles to come under Torah's yoke. This would be to make them slaves in a covenant which not only was never intended for them, but further, would seal them into a covenant whose grace has been withdrawn.

Yet the end of Torah's hegemony does not mean a free rein for lawlessness. While Torah as a covenant belongs to the old age of the flesh, this does not mean that all commandments are simply done away. No, for the advent of Christ means the advent of the Spirit who writes God's law upon the heart. The reign of Christ means liberation from both the guilt and dominion of Sin, and therefore God's new people will be characterized by holiness in a fashion that God's Torah-people never could have been. While the former covenant has come to its end, its content has been taken up anew and glorified by being refracted through the great eschatological event of Christ and the Spirit, with the result that Gentiles who by nature do not have the law have come to fulfill the law.

Meanwhile, we continue to echo Peter: Paul remains difficult to understand. But we press forward, confident that within the complex maze of corridors and twisting shafts in Paul's thought, inestimable riches wait to be mined, and no labour is comparable in value to the gold that we seek there. For Paul's proclamation is the rich gospel of Jesus Christ.

Bibliography

Works Cited

Ames, William. *The Marrow of Theology*. John Dykstra Eusden, trans. Grand Rapids: Baker 1997 (1968).

Bahnsen, Greg. *Theonomy in Christian Ethics*. Phillipsburg, NJ: Presbyterian and Reformed, 1977.

Bauer, Walter. *A Greek-English Lexicon of the New Testament and Other Early Christian Literature*. 3rd ed. Edited and revised by W. F. Arndt, F. W. Gingrich, and F. W. Danker. Chicago: University of Chicago Press, 2000 (1957).

Beker, J. Christiaan. *Paul the Apostle: The Triumph of God in Life and Thought*. Philadelphia: Fortress, 1980.

Bekken, Per Jarle. "Paul's Use of Deut 30,12-14 in Jewish Context: Some Observations." In *The New Testament and Hellenistic Judaism*, pp. 183-203. Edited by Peder Borden and Soren Giversen. Peabody, MS: Hendrickson, 1997 (1995).

Braswell, Joseph P. "'The Blessing of Abraham' Versus 'The Curse of the Law': Another Look at Gal 3:10-13." *Westminster Theological Journal*, 53:73-91 (1991).

Bruce, F. F. *The Epistle to the Galatians*. The New International Greek Testament Commentary. Edited by I. Howard Marshall and Donald A. Hagner. Grand Rapids: Eerdmans, 1998 (1982).

Bunyan, John. *Justification by an Imputed Righteousness*. Choteau, MT: Old Paths, n.d.

Calvin, John. "Commentaries on the Epistle to the Romans." In *Calvin's Commentaries*, Volume XIX. Translated and edited by John Owen. Grand Rapids: Baker, 1998 (English translation 1849; original publication 1539).

_____. *Institutes of the Christian Religion*. Ford Lewis Battles, trans.; John T. McNeil, ed. Philadelphia: Westminster, 1960.

Carson, D. A.; Peter T. O'Brien; and Mark A. Seifrid, eds. *Justification and Variegated Nomism: Volume 1 - The Complexities of Second Temple Judaism*. Grand Rapids: Baker Academic, 2001.

Catechism of the Catholic Church: With Modifications from the Editio Typica. No author. New York: Doubleday/Image, 1997.

Dunn, James D. G. *The Acts of the Apostles. Narrative Commentaries*. Ivor H. Jones, gen. ed. Valley Forge, PN: Trinity Press International, 1996.

_____. *Romans 1-8. Word Biblical Commentary*, vol. 38a. Bruce M. Metzger, gen. ed. Dallas: Word, 1988.

_____. *The Epistle to the Galatians. Black's New Testament Commentary*. Henry Chadwick, gen. ed. Peabody, MA: Hendrickson, 1993.

_____. *The Theology of Paul the Apostle*. Grand Rapids: Eerdmans, 1998.

Fee, Gordon D. *God's Empowering Presence: The Holy Spirit in the Letters of Paul*.

Gaffin, Richard B. Jr. *Resurrection and Redemption: A Study in Paul's Soteriology*. Phillipsburg, NJ: P & R, 1987 (1978).

Gallant, Tim. "Abraham's One True Heir? Galatians 3.16 and Identity Interchange." Online: http://www.rabbisaul.com/articles/oneseed.php

_____. "Covenantal Nomism? A Critical Review of E. P. Sanders, Paul and Palestinian Judaism, and D. A. Carson et al, Justification and Variegated Nomism, Vol. 1." Online: http://www.rabbisaul.com/articles/nomism.php

_____. "Fulfillment in the Gospel of Matthew." Online: http://www.biblicalstudiescenter.org/interpretation/fulfillment.php

_____. "Last Days Justification: Galatians 2.16 in Biblical and Occasional Context." Online: http://www.rabbisaul.com/articles/gal2_lastdaysjustification.php

_____. "Reform for the Sake of Reformation: My Agenda In Pauline Studies, Such As It Is - An *Apologia*." Online: http://www.rabbisaul.com/apologia.php

_____. "What Saint Paul Should Have Said." Online: http://www.rabbisaul.com/articles/shouldhave.php

Garlington, Don. *Exposition of Galatians: A New Perspective/Reformational Reading*. Eugene, OR: Wipf and Stock, 2003.

Gathercole, Simon J. *Where is Boasting? Early Jewish Soteriology and Paul's Response in Romans 1-5*. Grand Rapids: Eerdmans, 2002.

Hafemann, Scott J. *Paul, Moses, and the History of Israel*. Peabody, MA: Hendrickson, 1995.

Hays, Richard B. *The Faith of Jesus Christ: The Narrative Substructure of Galatians 3:1-4:11*. 2nd ed. Grand Rapids: Eerdmans, 2002 (1983).

Hegg, Tim. "Can We Speak of 'Law in the New Testament in Monolithic Terms?" ETS paper. Online:http://www.torahresource.com/English%20Articles/OrTorET S.pdf

Hodge, Charles. *Commentary on the Epistle to the Romans*. Grand Rapids: Eerdmans, 1993 (1886).

Jordan, James B. "The New Testament and the Dietary Laws." *Studies in Food and Faith*, no. 12. Niceville, FL: Biblical Horizons, 1990.

_____. "The Ten Words and Their Liturgical Usage." Rite Reasons 79 (August 2001). Niceville, FL: Biblical Horizons, 2001.

Josephus, Flavius. *Antiquities of the Jews*.

Leithart, Peter J. "'Judge Me, O God': Biblical Perspectives on Justification." In *The Federal Vision*, pp. 203-35. Monroe, LA: Athanasius, 2004.

Lusk, Rich. "Getting the Galatian Heresy Right." Online: http://www.hornes.org/theologia/content/rich_lusk/getting_the_galati an_heresy_right.htm

Luther, Martin. *Lectures on Galatians 1535: Chapters 1-4*. In *Luther's Works*, Vol. 26. Edited by Jaroslav Pelikan. Saint Louis: Concordia, 1963.

McGrath, Alister E. *Iustitia Dei: A History of the Christian Doctrine of Justification*. 2nd ed. Cambridge: Cambridge University Press, 1998 (1986).

Moo, Douglas J. "'Law,' 'Works of the Law,' and Legalism in Paul." *Westminster Theological Journal*, 45:73-100 (1983).

Murray, John. *The Epistle to the Romans. The New International Commentary on the New Testament*. F. F. Bruce, gen. ed. Grand Rapids: Eerdmans, 1990 (1959).

_____. *Redemption Accomplished and Applied*. Grand Rapids: Eerdmans, 1955.

Piper, John. *Counted Righteous in Christ: Should We Abandon the Imputation of Christ's Righteousness?* Wheaton, IL: Crossway, 2002.

Poythress, Vern. *The Shadow of Christ in the Law of Moses*. Brentwood, TN: Wolgemuth & Hyatt, 1991.

Räisänen, Heikki. *Paul and the Law*. Philadelphia: Fortress, 1986 (1983).

Ridderbos, Herman. *Paul: An Outline of His Theology*. Grand Rapids: Eerdmans, 1975 (1966).

Sanders, E. P. *Paul and Palestinian Judaism: A Comparison of Patterns of Religion*. Minneapolis: Fortress Press, 1977.

_____. *Paul, the Law, and the Jewish People*. Minneapolis: Fortress, 1983.

Schreiner, Thomas R. *Paul, Apostle of God's Glory in Christ: A Pauline Theology*. Downers Grove, IL: InterVarsity, 2001.

_____. *Romans. Baker Exegetical Commentary on the New Testament*. Edited by Moisés Silva. Grand Rapids: Baker, 1998.

Segal, Alan F. *Paul the Convert: The Apostolate and Apostasy of Saul the Pharisee*. New Haven, CT: Yale, 1990.

Turretin, Francis. *Institutes of Elenctic Theology*, Volume 2. George Musgrave Giger, trans. James T. Dennison, Jr., ed. Phillipsburg, NJ: P & R, 1994.

Vos, Geerhardus. *The Pauline Eschatology*. Grand Rapids: Eerdmans, 1972 (1930).

Ward, Rowland S. *God and Adam: Reformed Theology and the Creation Covenant*. Wantirna, Australia: New Melbourne Press, 2003.

Westerholm, Stephen. *Perspectives Old and New on Paul: The "Lutheran" Paul and His Critics*. Grand Rapids: Eerdmans, 2004.

Wilkins, Steve, and Duane Garner, eds. *The Federal Vision: A Collection of Essays on the Covenant*. Monroe, LA: Athanasius, 2004.

Witherington, Ben III. *Grace in Galatia: A Commentary on Paul's Letter to the Galatians*. Grand Rapids: Eerdmans, 1998.

Wright, N. T. *The Climax of the Covenant: Christ and the Law in Pauline Theology*. Minneapolis: Fortress, 1991.

_____. *Colossians and Philemon. Tyndale New Testament Commentaries*. Leon Morris, gen. ed. Grand Rapids: Eerdmans, 1986.

_____. *The Letter to the Romans*. In *The New Interpreter's Bible*, Vol. X. Leander Keck, convener and New Testament ed. Nashville, TN: Abingdon, 2002.

_____. *The New Testament and the People of God*. Minneapolis: Fortress, 1992.

Further Reference

In addition to the works cited above, valuable information relating to Paul and the law can be gleaned from the following sources, as well as the standard commentaries:

Dunn, James D. G., ed. *Paul and the Mosaic Law*. Grand Rapids: Eerdmans, 2001.

Kim, Seyoon. *Paul and the New Perspective: Second Thoughts on the Origin of Paul's Gospel*. Grand Rapids: Eerdmans, 2002.

Schreiner, Thomas. *The Law and its Fulfillment: A Pauline Theology of the Law*. Grand Rapids: Baker, 1993.

Stuhlmacher, Peter. *Revisiting Paul's Doctrine of Justification: A Challenge to the New Perspective*. Downers Grove, IL: Inter-Varsity, 2001.

Thielman, Frank. *Paul and the Law: A Contextual Approach*. Downers Grove, IL: Inter-Varsity, 1994.

Thompson, Michael B. *The New Perspective on Paul*. Grove Biblical Series B 26. Cambridge: Grove, 2002.

Wright, N. T. *What Saint Paul Really Said: Was Paul of Tarsus the Real Founder of Christianity?* Grand Rapids: Eerdmans, 1997.

Mini-Glossary

Aeon. An age or era, particularly having to do with fundamental newness, such that the differing eras are like "different worlds."

Cosmic, cosmos, kosmos. The Greek term *kosmos* refers to the ordered world in its totality. The language fits the biblical idea of the heavens and the earth.

Eschatology. A theological term referring to the doctrine of the last things. In biblical studies usage, it frequently refers to how much of the Old Testament anticipation had to do with "the latter days." The coming new covenant was not simply another stop on the road of redemptive history; it was an eschatological hope.

Nomos. The Greek term usually translated "law." In Paul, it almost always refers either to the Mosaic covenant or to the Old Testament as Scripture. The Hebrew equivalent is *Torah*.

Stoicheia. Elements. The Greek term originally referred to the elements which constituted material reality, such as earth, air/wind, water, fire. Paul uses the term to refer to the elements that constituted the old world (*aeon*, see above).

Scripture Index

About the Author

Tim Gallant has served in the pastorate for several years. He graduated with honours from Mid-America Reformed Seminary in Dyer, Indiana (2000). A highlight of his seminary work was an extensive two-part paper (equivalent to about 200 double-spaced pages) comprised of a commentary on Galatians 3 and a passage-by-passage overview of Paul's view of the law.

Tim is the author of *Feed My Lambs: Why the Lord's Table Should Be Restored to Covenant Children,* as well as dozens of biblical and theological articles. He also contributed essays to *The Case for Covenant Communion* (Gregg Strawbridge, ed.) and *The Glory of Kings* (Peter Leithart and John Barach, eds.), a festschrift for James B. Jordan.

Tim does branding, graphic arts, and web site development (through Tim Gallant Creative), and currently serves as an elder in Christ Covenant Church of Grande Prairie. He and his wife Kristi thrive on the joy and hard work of raising eight children.

www.ingramcontent.com/pod-product-compliance
Lightning Source LLC
Chambersburg PA
CBHW071639050426

42443CB00026B/766